Anonymous

The Local Government Act

A series of explanatory articles, reprinted from the Times

Anonymous

The Local Government Act
A series of explanatory articles, reprinted from the Times

ISBN/EAN: 9783337252380

Printed in Europe, USA, Canada, Australia, Japan

Cover: Foto ©Suzi / pixelio.de

More available books at **www.hansebooks.com**

THE
LOCAL GOVERNMENT ACT.

A Series of Explanatory Articles,

Reprinted from

The Times.

PRICE SIXPENCE.

LONDON :
PRINTED AND PUBLISHED BY GEORGE EDWARD WRIGHT, AT
THE TIMES OFFICE, PRINTING-HOUSE SQUARE.

1888.

THE LOCAL GOVERNMENT ACT.

I.—THE NEW ORDER OF THINGS.

The nature of the legislative alterations in local government may be known, but will hardly be fully appreciated until the county councils have been elected, have got settled in the saddle, and have been intrusted with the higher powers foreshadowed by the Act. The readers of *The Times* have had the opportunity of reading the Local Government (England and Wales) Act, 1888, in full. Yet even those who have availed themselves of that opportunity, and still more those who have not done so, may be glad to have stated as concisely as may be the nature of the change that is effected. It is important that both the county electors and intending candidates should be precisely informed on this point. The changes contemplated by the Local Government Bill were so far-reaching and so extensive that, omitting the larger boroughs, every sanitary and highway authority would have been remodelled, and its duties and powers would have been re-arranged. But circumstances did not permit of

the Bill passing in its original form. The provisions constituting district councils and assign-
ing their duties and powers had to be omitted,
and so a grant has been made to the chaos of
minor authorities of a new lease, but, as may be
hoped, a short one. Mr. Goschen's well-known
assertion that in one parish he had received
eight rate-papers for an aggregate demand of
12s. 4d. will be possible of repetition. The ratepayer must look forward to the future for a con-
centration in one authority of the powers and
duties now devolving upon numerous and
variously-elected local bodies. It cannot be too
distinctly insisted upon that the only new
authorities created by the Local Government
Act are the county councils. To these county
councils are intrusted all the administrative
duties that have hitherto devolved on the justices
in quarter sessions, and they have also a
qualified power of supervision in certain
sanitary matters. In all county matters representation and taxation are to go hand in hand.
Local taxation is, moreover, to be relieved.
While some grants from the Imperial exchequer
are discontinued, other sources of revenue are
handed over, and local taxation is to receive a
net benefit of some £3,000,000 annually. Thus,
while the Legislature has set up new local authorities, it has started them fairly on their way by
giving them the means of substantially reducing
the rates which it is necessary should be levied.

The new bodies, then, created by the Act are
the county councils, which are to be elected next
January, and which will enter upon their duties
in April. To these councils the Act relegates
" all the administrative business of the justices
in quarter sessions." So the ratepayer who pays
the piper will to some extent be able to call

the tune. The question, for instance, of providing a new lunatic asylum, at a cost perhaps of £200,000 or £300,000, will have to be considered and decided, not by a body of gentlemen appointed to conserve the peace, but by the elected representatives of the ratepayers. This alone would be a change of grave importance. But the maintenance, management, and visitation of the pauper lunatic asylums will also devolve upon the county councils. They will have to maintain and to establish, when necessary, reformatory and industrial schools. In all these matters a vast amount of patronage will devolve on the county councils. They will also be subject to the danger arising to all public bodies, of having to obtain considerable supplies, and, for that purpose, of having to enter into large and numerous contracts. This work has for the most part been carried on by the courts of quarter sessions by means of their committees. The committees have, of course, done their business in private; and once a quarter, and also annually, they have reported at quarter sessions what they have done. Elective bodies will not be able to carry out business of the kind in this unobtrusive, quiet way. There will be members of the county councils who will naturally feel that their constituents will want to know what is going on. They will expect that when they go up for re-election they will have to justify the engagement of Mr. A to supply goods for the county asylums which Mr. B was ready to offer at a lower price. If the fate of a Government has been known to tremble in the balance in respect of the alleged mistake of a police-constable, how much more likely is it that the re-election of a county councillor may be influenced by a single instance of ill-temper or indiscretion on the part of a lunatic asylum attendant! It is therefore probable that at a very early period of their existence we shall have debates at the county council meetings as to the maintenance and management of the county lunatic asylums. In those cases where the county councils, as elected, may consist entirely or almost entirely of members who are county magistrates, and who have been accustomed to work together in the courts of quarter sessions, the business will probably be conducted on the same lines as heretofore. But where new men, anxious to distinguish themselves, come from all parts of a county to the meetings of the county council, it is certain that discussion must take place, if only that the constituency may see what active and energetic representatives it has secured. If, then, we are to have debates, we may rest assured that the county councillors will take care that those debates are reported in the newspapers throughout the county. Eloquence in the council meetings will be thrown away and wasted unless it be reported in every corner of the constituency. And the reports of the council meetings will bring home to the county electors the fact that, through their representatives, they have a voice in the management of important and interesting business. It is business, too, which will be felt to be none the less interesting to the county elector because his village is represented, not only on the county council, but in the county lunatic asylum. There are, unhappily, but few villages in England which do not send their quota of patients to the county asylum. Many of the rural districts and villages are also represented in the reformatory and industrial schools, of which the establishment and maintenance are placed, as we have seen, in the hands of the county councils.

The Local Government Act, however, gives to the county councils other work as to which debates and discussions must arise. Licensing houses and other places for music and dancing will be a duty to test the real power of each county council, if, indeed, it should not give rise to an election cry upon which an election might turn. The courts of quarter sessions are never so crowded as when a vote is to be taken for or against the grant or renewal of a music and dancing licence. Such a question, if it excites the appointed justice, who is independent and careless of the *vox populi*, will surely exercise the elected of the people, whose seat may depend upon the result of a vote of the council. In a populous electoral district the renewal, or the refusal of the county council to renew, an important music and dancing licence might easily gain or lose a county councillor's seat. The execution of the Acts relating to the contagious diseases of animals will be another subject upon which the elected of the people will feel the pressure of public opinion more directly than it has been felt by the county justices. The closure of a market or the suspension of a fair may sometimes be all-important in the general interest of the county, while it may mean temporary stagnation to the special trade or business of a small town or village. Such questions as this will often come before the county council, and will, no doubt, be decided as seems most likely to insure the greatest good to the greatest number. Yet the county councillor will not be able to forget the special interests of his constituents, nor the fact that they may sometimes conflict with the general interests of the rest of the county. The appointment, removal, and determination of

the salaries of the county treasurer, county
surveyor, medical officer of health, and other
minor officials will from time to time exercise the county councils, and will give rise to
energetic discussion, in which the penny wise and
the pound foolish as well as the true economists
will make their voices heard. And such matters
as these will, when reported, be rediscussed with no
less vigour by our respected friend Hodge and his
neighbours at the time-honoured but informal
meetings which are held throughout our rural
districts once or oftener every week at the village
inns. The candidate for the office of county
coroner will never again have to canvass the
freeholders of the county, for the appointment
to that office is placed in the hands of the
county council. There is one piece of valuable
patronage with which the county council is not
intrusted. That, oddly enough, is the appointment of their own clerk. For the sake, no doubt,
of avoiding compensation the Act provides that
the existing clerks of the peace shall be clerks
to the county councils. This arrangement has
its disadvantages. The chief executive officer
will hold his appointment independently of his
council. He, moreover, will probably entertain
a strong conviction that the lines upon which the
county business has been transacted in the past
are the only lines upon which it can safely be
transacted in the future. Among their own
members the county councils will be able to
confer various distinctions. They will appoint
their chairman and vice-chairman. They will
be able to elect county aldermen, who may or
may not have submitted themselves to the
suffrages of the electors, and they will have to
appoint representatives of the council to serve
on a joint committee composed of members of the

council and of quarter sessions justices for the purposes of police, and who will have the appointment of future clerks of the peace and other joint officers.

While the powers and duties to which reference has already been made should suffice to attract good men and true to the council table, there are other matters to be dealt with of equal or even greater importance. The county councils, while they may themselves appoint for their own consultation and assistance a medical officer of health, are to receive from all the districts in the county copies of the reports made by the district medical officers of health to the district bodies. If it should then appear to the county council from any such report that the Public Health Act has not been properly put in force in the district to which the report relates, or that any other matter affecting the public health of the district requires to be remedied, the council may cause a representation to be made to the Local Government Board on the matter. Moreover, the council have power to enforce the provisions of the Rivers Pollution Prevention Act. The importance of these two enactments can hardly be over-estimated. The local authority of a small area is too often without the strength of mind and without the necessary public confidence to enable it to carry into execution adequate though necessary measures of sanitary reform. Local and sometimes unworthy influences are frequently too strong for the would-be reformers, and the new Act therefore, in setting up a superior authority in every county, will have conferred an enormous boon upon many a suffering and still insanitary district. Such powers as these will, however, tax the independence and public spirit of the county councillors, and may in many instances bring them into conflict with the limited public opinion of some of the districts that may be affected. These powers are the more interesting to consider in that they are almost the only instances in the new Act of positive decentralization, an operation for which Mr. Ritchie told the House of Commons there was an urgent demand throughout the country. Another important power conferred for the first time upon a county authority is that of opposing Bills in Parliament and of prosecuting or defending legal proceedings necessary for the promotion or protection of the interests of the inhabitants of the county. Such powers as these bring to mind innumerable instances in which, for want of *locus standi*, courts of quarter sessions have been unable to appear before Parliament, while the small local authorities have not been able to combine effectually.

The exercise by the county councils of their financial powers will tax the capacity for business of the county councillors, and will probably do much to enable the county ratepayer to realize the effect of the change wrought by the Act. Many of the municipal corporations have been able to relieve the ratepayer of the present generation by extending the term over which the capital expenditure has had to be repaid. In this respect the emasculation which the Local Government Bill suffered in its progress through Committee is probably to be regretted. The Bill proposed that the term over which the repayment of loans was to be spread should not exceed 60 years. In Committee the period was reduced to 30 years. It may be doubted whether this reduction of term would have been proposed if the nature and practical operation of municipal and local finance had been really understood.

Neither county councils nor municipal corporations have any means of raising, except by loan, the funds necessary for capital or permanent expenditure. For the construction of our railways, docks, and other commercial undertakings the capital needed is raised by issuing shares. It may well be doubted if the London and North-Western Railway would be now in existence if it had been a condition precedent to raising its capital that the whole sum should be repaid out of revenue within the first 30 years of the existence of the company. Yet this is an instance of the principle insisted upon by those who argue that the debts incurred by local bodies for permanent works should be discharged within a limited time. It may readily be conceded that it would be imprudent and, indeed, dishonest if the county council of one year were to be at liberty to incur heavy liabilities for current and evanescent purposes and to leave the discharge of their current debts to their successors of the following year. But the case is altered when money is spent in the purchase of land and the erection of buildings of ever-increasing value. There is in such a case no real necessity that the expenditure shall be discharged in 30 rather than in 40 years, nor in 40 rather than in 50 years. The fair and reasonable way of meeting such a case is to do as the Local Government Board is daily called upon to do—viz., to fix the period for repayment after consideration of the probable period of duration of the benefit of the particular work. However, the Act as passed limits the period of repayment to 30 years in the case of a new loan and in the case of reborrowing to the period of the original sanction. But as before the Act the justices of some of our counties had already sought to emulate the example set by the municipal corporations and to convert their loans into stock, so many of the county councils will doubtless, upon their accession to office, turn their attention to the question of existing loans, and see whether, by creating county stock, they may not be able both to reduce the rate of interest and to extend the term over which the loans are being repaid. The justices of Essex not very long since obtained special legislative powers in this direction, and last Session the Surrey justices introduced a Bill, which they only withdrew in view of the changes contemplated by the Local Government Act, then passing through Parliament. But whether the county councils set their houses in order in this respect or not, the transferred licences and probate duty grant should enable a substantial reduction to be made in local taxation generally. Indeed, it will be obvious that the £3,000,000 handed over out of the Imperial Exchequer must, in one way or another, help the local ratepayer.

Hitherto reference has only been made to the changes actually effected by the Act itself or likely to flow from its operation. When the contemplated further powers are transferred from the Local Government Board and the Board of Trade to the county councils, then these bodies will become of still more importance and will be far more powerful than they are as immediately created by the Act. They are, in fact, huge machines capable not only of doing their own work, but of furnishing the motive power for the vast and complicated mechanism that must exist throughout all the country districts of England and Wales. By the Bill it was proposed at once to transfer certain important powers to the county councils. But in Committee these powers were struck out, and it was left to the Local Government Board to transfer these and other powers by provisional order. Indeed, the county councils may have transferred to them all such powers, duties, and liabilities of the Privy Council, of the Board of Trade, Local Government Board, Education Department, Secretary of State, or Government Department as are " conferred by statute and appear to relate to matters arising within the county and to be of an administrative character." Thus the county councils may, without further legislative action, become really county parliaments. They may have power to authorize the construction of public works, and, for that purpose, to empower the compulsory acquirement of land. They may be invested with the control and supervision of the sanitary authorities, the boards of guardians, and the School Boards in their counties. Thus, by the order of the Local Government Board, the Act may really operate as a decentralizing measure, and the county councils may acquire a position of commanding influence and authority which cannot fail to attract the best men in the counties as candidates for the honour of membership. Even, however, if no order should ever be made by the Local Government Board in this direction, and if the minor local authorities should continue to revel in their chaotic confusion of area and conflict of jurisdiction, the change in the system of county government effected by the new Act will suffice to make the passage of the Act through Parliament a notable era in the history of local government. The actual powers conferred upon the county councils will, moreover, be quite sufficient to give them prestige enough to induce the candidature of men who will feel that their real right to represent their neighbours depends not

only on the popular cry of the moment, but on
the permanent and enduring success of the
operations of the council at whose table they
sit.

II.—THE GOVERNMENT OF LONDON.

It is seldom that a legislative change of equal magnitude and importance to the extinction of the Metropolitan Board of Works and the transfer of its powers and property to a successor has been accomplished in as few words as those which effected this operation in the Local Government Act, 1888. "After the appointed day the Metropolitan Board of Works shall cease to exist" is the simple method adopted by the draftsman of the Act for performing the happy despatch. Nor was Mr. Ritchie himself very ceremonious on the subject of the Metropolitan Board of Works when he introduced the Bill to the House of Commons. There was almost a sensation in the House when, in reply to a question as to what would become of the Metropolitan Board of Works, Mr. Ritchie simply said, "It will cease to exist." Rumours had for some days been industriously circulated that the Local Government Bill would not touch the metropolis; but by the expedient of treating London in much the same way as the rest of England, the Government at one stroke got rid of the Metropolitan Board of Works, and substituted for it a directly-elected body. Mr. Ritchie had evidently not felt himself in the dilemma suggested somewhat tersely by a *Quarterly* Reviewer, who put the problem of the local

government of London as involving the difficulty
either of " absolutely annihilating the City on
the one hand, or of subjecting the whole of the
metropolis to the rule of Gog and Magog."
Under the Local Government Act the City is by
no means annihilated, while the government of
Gog and Magog is in no way extended. Indeed,
the territory of Gog and Magog is almost left
alone. The Livery of the City of London are
deprived of the privilege of electing a Sheriff for
Middlesex, and Her Majesty is to appoint the
Sheriff for the County of London. The Common
Council have taken away from them the power of
electing their Common Serjeant, while future
Recorders are not to exercise judicial duties
until duly appointed thereto by Her Majesty.
The powers and duties of the Court of Quarter
Sessions and Justices of the City are divided
between the Court of Common Council and the
County Council. But practically, with the excep-
tions mentioned, the Act will not effect any serious
change in the local management of the City of
London, and the Commissioners of Sewers will
still remain the sanitary authority within the
City boundaries.

Although comprised in a few words, the enactments of the Local Government Act with regard
to the government of the metropolis are of vast
and far-reaching importance. The operation of
the change effected will best be appreciated by
an examination of the powers and duties of the
present governing bodies, and by a slight
reference to the inheritance, from a financial point
of view, to which the County Council of London
will succeed. The position and the powers of
the vestries and district boards of the metropolis
undergo no change, except that these bodies will
no longer elect the members of the Metropolitan

Board of Works. They will still remain charged with the maintenance and construction of local sewers ; they will still have to pave, light, scavenge, and water streets ; they will still have to see to the abatement of nuisances and the removal of dust. It is reserved for the future to transfer these powers and duties to district councils, the members of which shall be elected by a body of electors corresponding to the burgesses of a municipal borough. None of these duties of detail have hitherto been discharged by the Metropolitan Board of Works ; the operations of that body have been confined to works of greater magnitude, if not of more importance. The Metropolitan Board have had the management of all public works in which the ratepayers of the metropolis had a common interest. They were charged when first established with the maintenance of the main sewers, with the execution of works for intercepting and diverting sewage from the Thames. They were empowered to make, widen, and improve streets, and to effect general objects for the public benefit. They had control over the construction of local sewers by the vestries and district boards, and they had power to regulate the projection of buildings beyond the general line of frontage, the height of buildings, and the width of streets. The Acts of Parliament under which they have carried out the various duties devolving upon them are nearly 100 in number, and confer extensive and general powers. The Metropolitan Board is the local authority for the metropolis under the Acts relating to explosives, artisans' dwellings, the contagious diseases of animals, tramways, slaughter-houses, and petroleum, and they have also financial powers far beyond those which will attach to the county councils in general under the Local Government Act. They are, for instance, authorized to lend to the London School Board and local bodies throughout the metropolis such sums as they may require for capital expenditure. In this way the Metropolitan Board have now outstanding loans due to them for upwards of £8,000,000, which the different local authorities are paying off by regular contributions, with interest. The Metropolitan Board have from time to time been authorized to free and to combine in freeing some of the toll-bridges over the Thames. They have under their control parks, gardens, and open spaces to an extent of upwards of 2,600 acres, and the improvements that they have under various Acts, from time to time, carried out, such as the construction of the Thames Embankments, the formation of Queen Victoria-street and Northumberland-avenue, besides many other very important new thoroughfares in the metropolis, will give some idea of the magnitude of the operations which in the future may devolve upon the County Council of London. In addition, however, to the work which has been performed by the Metropolitan Board of Works, the new County Council has, under the Local Government Act, transferred to it business of considerable importance. It has the provision, maintenance, management, and visitation of asylums for pauper lunatics. It will have to maintain and establish reformatory and industrial schools. It will have the licensing of houses and places for music and dancing, and the grant of licences of such racecourses as are within the metropolis and within ten miles of Charing-cross. Besides all this, the County Council will exercise extensive financial powers, and will have to make and levy county rates. It will have the charge of bridges, hitherto vested in the county authority. It will elect the coroner, and will besides have full powers of appointing and dismissing a large army of officials. The County Council of London will also have power to enforce the provisions of the Rivers Pollution Prevention Act, 1876. They may appoint a medical officer of health, before whom the medical officers of the districts in London will have to lay their annual reports. Thus, for the first time, a central authority in London will have some general supervision of the health statistics. This is a power which has not yet existed, except so far as the Metropolitan Asylums Board—who, as is well known, have charge of the infectious hospitals of the metropolis—have found it necessary to consider the public health of London in regard to the probable accommodation wanted for persons suffering from infectious disease. Besides all these powers, the Local Government Board may in the future, by provisional order, transfer to the County Council of London any of the powers, duties, and liabilities of an administrative character which at present are vested in various Government departments, and may relate to matters arising within the county.

The inheritance of liability to which the London County Council will succeed is of considerable magnitude. It appears from the statement of accounts of the Metropolitan Board for the year ending December 31, 1887, that at that date there was an outstanding indebtedness of £28,000,000. On the other hand, the Metropolitan Asylums Board, the London School Board, and district boards owed the Metropolitan Board of Works £3,400,000 ; and surplus land, money lent, money due upon precepts, cash in hand, and other assets brought up the credit side of the capital account to £11,400,000. A brief abstract of the receipts and payments by the Board during the last year for which the accounts have been published will give some idea of the annual receipts and payments that will come within the ken of the London County Council :—

RECEIPTS.		PAYMENTS.	
Balances	£201,648	Interest of debt	£921,266
Raised by rates	960,653	Loans repaid	128,856
Coal and wine duties ..	320,974	Loans advanced by the Board	692,078
Contribution to Fire Brigade	36,227	Maintenance of sewers and expenses of pumping stations	137,328
Interest on loans and balances	306,902	Thames Embankment maintenance	12,945
Rents and deposits ..	92,152		
Fees	9,401	Hydrants	11,692
Sales of land, old materials, and return of deposits	143,538	Parks and open spaces	112,697
		Bridges	9,087
Loans raised	500,316	Establishment expenses	45,756
Loans repaid	310,119	Capital expenditure on improvements	572,920
Treasury Bills sold ..	1,143,737		
Sundry receipts	11,657	Main drainage and main sewers	222,251
		Fire Brigade stations and plant	14,330
		Contributions towards local improvements ..	43,800
		Investment in Treasury Bills	696,824
		Sundry expenses ..	55,000
		Balance carried forward	358,983
	£4,037,434		£4,037,434

These figures are only given to afford some general notion of the nature of the financial operations of the Metropolitan Board. The accounts of the County Council will certainly be different in some respects, and possibly in many. The item of receipts from coal and wine duties will not appear on the credit side of the account, and, on the other hand, the County Council of London will receive the transferred licences, amounting, as it was estimated by the Local Government Board, to £427,000, and in proportion to the existing grants they will receive out of the probate duty grant £428,000. If the division of the probate duty grant had taken place on the basis originally contemplated, the metropolis would have been entitled to £536,000 ; but as it is they will only receive the sum mentioned. Out of these moneys the County Council will have to make good the Parliamentary grants towards the remuneration of Poor Law medical officers, &c., and will have to give the guardians of the Poor Law unions which are wholly within the metropolis an amount equal to 4d. per head per day for every indoor pauper maintained in their unions, the Act containing provisions as to the mode in which the number of indoor paupers is to be ascertained. This amount, however, it is expressly provided, is to be an addition to any payment made out of the Metropolitan Poor Law Fund.

The charge of the main sewers of London is, as may well be imagined, a source of constant anxiety. The total length of the sewers which will fall under the charge of the London County Council is about 250 miles, and the cleansing involves the employment of 124 men, at an annual cost of about £15,500. An experiment that was tried for some time of endeavouring to deodorize the sewage in the sewers by mixing permanganate of soda with the sewage was found exceedingly expensive, and is reported by the Board of Works to have been discontinued. Whenever complaints are now received of offensive odours arising from any of the ventilating shafts to the Board's sewers, sulphurous acid is applied. During 12 months this only cost £600. and the

result is stated to have been " not unsatis-
factory." But at the outfalls a large quantity of
permanganate of soda has been used, and during
95 days the deodorizing operations there cost no
less than £42,000. The management of the
Metropolitan Fire Brigade is also a duty that
will fall upon the London County Council, and
in this, as well as in many other matters, the
ratepayers will doubtless feel the benefit of a
directly representative body coming to the work,
and being under no obligation to run in the same
grooves as their predecessors. The present strength
of the Metropolitan Fire Brigade is stated at 674,
and the annual expenditure for one year was
£112,000. Of this £77,000 was contributed by
the ratepayers, £26,000 by insurance companies,
and the balance by contributions from the
Treasury and by expenses recovered. In addition
to this expenditure, the County Council will
have to provide hydrants for the extinction of
fires. Altogether the expenditure of the Council
towards the extinction of fires in the metropolis
will amount to about £100,000. The quality
of the gas will have to be looked after by the
Council, and that the Metropolitan Board have
always taken an interest in the water supply of
the metropolis is well known. The Parliamentary work in connexion with the metropolis is
considerable. Railway and tramway Bills are
usually presented in considerable numbers to
Parliament, and not only is the consent of the
Board sometimes necessary as the local authority
of the metropolis, but they have been in the habit
of watching these Bills through Parliament and
of obtaining restrictive provisions intended in the
interest of the ratepayers. Then the administration of the Contagious Diseases (Animals) Acts is
almost a business of itself. During one year

the Metropolitan Board had to slaughter 262 beasts, to the value of £4,700 ; and a number of swine were also slaughtered on account of typhoid or swine fever. The care of cowsheds and dairies will devolve upon the London County Council, as well as the inspection of the premises of about 750 cowkeepers, with something like 10,000 cows ; the inspection of slaughter-houses, numbering in the metropolis 742, and the supervision of such offensive businesses as those of knackers, tripe-boilers, bone-boilers, soap-boilers, &c. The manufacture, conveyance, storage, and sale of explosives will also be one of the matters to exercise the London Council. During one year 1,300 tons of explosives were dealt with by the inspectors of the Metropolitan Board, and no fewer than 3,357 premises are registered for keeping explosives, and are constantly examined by the inspectors of the Board. The keepers of petroleum, too, have to register their premises with the Board, and have to undergo inspection, and during one year 1,656 licences of this kind were granted. Then, under the Infant Life Protection Act, it is not lawful for any person to receive for hire to nurse it apart from its parents more than one infant, except in a house registered by the local authority, which would be the County Council, and that authority has power to fix the number of infants which may be received, and, indeed, may refuse to register the house unless the house be suitable or unless satisfied of the good character of the person applying for registration. Under this Act there are at present only 19 registered houses in the metropolis, and 103 infants are kept at them. It will thus be seen that not only large questions of principle will have to be dealt with by the London County Council, but that there will be a

considerable amount of detail work devolve upon
it, although an enormous mass of details must
daily come before the vestries and district boards.

It may be well, before passing to consider the
composition of the Metropolitan Board of Works
and its mode of election as compared with that of
the London County Council, to refer briefly to
the vestries and district boards. The general
nature of the duties devolving upon them has
already been mentioned. When the first
Act was passed, in 1855, dealing with the
constitution of the Metropolitan Board of
Works and the general local government of
the metropolis, it was provided that 23 of the
larger parishes of the metropolis should each
have their own separate system of local administration under vestries, and the smaller parishes
and places were grouped into districts and were
to be managed by district boards. The number
of vestrymen was fixed at 18 for every parish in
which the householders should not exceed 1,000,
and six additional vestrymen up to 2,000, and 12
additional vestrymen for every further 1,000; but
they were not to exceed 120 in all. It was provided that the incumbent and churchwardens
should be members of the vestry. The district
boards, to look after the local affairs of districts
combined to large parishes, however, were to be
elected by the vestries of the parishes in combination. Thus, while the vestries were subject
to direct election, the district boards were
elected through the vestries of the constituent
parishes ; thus ratepayers who were desirous of
serving on a district board had often to run the
gauntlet of being elected to a select vestry in the
first instance.

The rates levied by the vestries and district
boards seem to vary considerably. The Metro-

politan Board of Works have from time to time, in their annual reports, published a table showing the rate raised for metropolitan and local purposes in each parish in the metropolis. No such table is to be found in the Metropolitan Board's Report for 1887, but the table published in the report for 1886 probably gives for all practical purposes a correct idea of the great discrepancies that exist. The following table gives the average annual rate in the pound for the five years from 1882 to 1886, and it will be seen that the rate varies from a *maximum* of 6s. 7d. to a *minimum* of 3s. 9d. The figures quoted include the Poor rate, the general rate, the School Board and lighting rates, the sewers rate, and the Metropolitan Consolidated rate :—

	s.	d.		s.	d.
St. Marylebone	4	9	Clapham	5	7
St. Pancras	4	9	Tooting Graveney	6	5
Lambeth	5	5	Streatham	5	2
St. George, Hanover-square	3	10	St. Mary, Battersea (excluding Penge)	5	0
Islington	4	4	Wandsworth	5	7
Shoreditch	4	11	Putney (including Roehampton)	5	9
Paddington	4	2			
Bethnal-green	6	3	Hackney	5	0
Newington	5	6	St. Mary, Stoke Newington	5	0
Camberwell	5	2			
St. James's, Westminster	3	9	St. Giles-in-the-Fields, St. George, Bloomsbury	5	4
Clerkenwell	5	5	St. Andrew, Holborn-above-Bars, St. George-the-Martyr	5	3
Chelsea	5	3			
Kensington	4	5			
St. Luke, Middlesex	6	1	St. Sepulchre, Middlesex	5	8
St. George, Southwark	5	8	Saffron-hill, &c.	5	9
Bermondsey	5	8	Liberty of Glasshouse-yard	4	0
St. George-in-the-East	5	10	St. Anne, Soho	4	4
St. Martin-in-the-Fields	3	8	St. Paul, Covent-garden	4	3
Mile-end Old-town	5	8	Precinct of the Savoy	4	3

	s. d.		s. d.
Woolwich	5 9	St. Mary-le-Strand ..	4 2
Rotherhithe..	5 8	St. Clement Danes ..	4 1
Hampstead	4 8	Liberty of the Rolls ..	4 1
Hammersmith	5 11	St. Anne, Limehouse ..	5 11
Fulham	5 8	St. John, Wapping ..	4 7
St. Mary, Whitechapel ..	5 6	St. Paul, Shadwell ..	5 10
Christchurch, Spitalfields	5 7	Hamlet of Ratcliff ..	5 4
St. Botolph without Ald-		All Saints, Poplar.. ..	5 8
gate	5 1	St. Mary,Stratford-le-Bow	6 1
Holy Trinity, Minories ..	5 9	St. Leonard, Bromley ..	6 4
Precinct of St. Katharine	4 10	Christchurch	5 1
Hamlet of Mile-end New-		St. Saviour	4 1
town	6 0	Charlton-next-Woolwich	6 7
Liberty of Norton Folgate	5 4	Plumstead	5 8
Old Artillery-ground ..	5 7	Eltham	5 10
District of the Tower ..	5 10	Lee	5 10
St. Margaret.. .. }	3 11	Kidbrooke	5 5
St. John the Evangelist }		Lewisham	5 3
St. Paul, Deptford, in-		Hamlet of Penge	5 1
cluding Hatcham ..	5 6	St. Olave	4 9
St. Nicholas, Deptford ..	5 0	St.Thomas,Southwark ..	4 8
Greenwich	6 2	St. John, Horselydown ..	4 9

Average Annual Rate in the £ .. .. 5s. 2d.

The interest attaching to the foregoing table
is that it illustrates the difficulty that may
exist in dealing with the details of local government of the metropolis when it may be
proposed to extinguish the vestries and the
district boards and to erect a new authority, or new authorities, to take their place. The
table almost seems to show that it will be necessary to allow each district which is now under
the control of a vestry or district board to
remain for local purposes of management in
detail a separate district under the jurisdiction
of a separate authority. Considerable agitation
would necessarily arise if a measure were pro-

posed by which an average rate for all local purposes should be struck throughout the whole of
the metropolis. The discrepancy which exists
is caused to some extent by differences in the
Poor rate arising from the peculiar local circumstances of different parishes, but this does not
account for all the discrepancies to be found.
In some cases expenditure on road-making,
mending, scavenging, and watering differs very
much, and a careful examination of the accounts
of the various vestries would seem to indicate
that differential rates are matters of necessity in
the several districts of London.

The constitution of the County Council for
London will be vastly different from that of the
Metropolitan Board of Works. One instance will
enable the reader to see how striking the con-
trast is. The ratepayers of Penge, one of the
outlying districts of the metropolis, meet and
elect a vestry. That vestry, in the course of
their duties, elect members to the Lewisham
Board of Works. In their turn the Lewisham
Board of Works elect a representative for their
district to the Metropolitan Board of Works.
Thus the mode of election of the expiring authority is about as indirect as it can possibly be.
The new County Council is to be very differently
chosen. The members are to be elected by a
new body of voters and by direct election. Each
of the Parliamentary boroughs comprised in the
metropolis is to return to the County Council of
London double the number of members which it
is entitled to send to the Imperial Parliament.
The metropolis now sends 59 members to the
House of Commons, and so the County Council
of London will consist of 118 elected members
and of 19 aldermen, for the aldermen in the
County of London are not to exceed one-sixth of

the number of councillors. The aldermen will be elected by the Council at a provisional meeting. In order that candidates and voters may have a precise notion of the districts that will be represented, and may have some idea of the numbers of the various electors, the following table is given, showing the Parliamentary boroughs in the metropolis, with the number of Parliamentary electors recorded at the last revision. It is not possible at present to give the number of county electors who will be entitled to vote in the election of county councillors for London, but it is probable that they will not differ seriously from the numbers given below. As a rule the number of burgesses in a municipal borough slightly exceeds the number of Parliamentary voters. The lodgers and the service voters who do not get the municipal franchise are generally less in number than the lady voters who have the privilege of assisting in the election of town and county councillors. The following table, then, shows the metropolitan boroughs and the numbers of Parliamentary voters. It may be added that each constituency will be entitled to two representatives on the County Council of London, with the exception of the City of London, which will have four representatives, whose voting power, however, will be limited :—

		No. of Voters.			No. of Voters.
Hampstead ..	.. ..	6,935	Twr. Hmlts., Mile-end ..		5,571
St. Pancras, North		6,190	„	Limehouse ..	6,272
„	West ..	7,261	„	Bow and Bromley	9,492
„	East ..	6,557	„	Poplar	9,340
„	South..	5,554	Fulham	.. .. ..	7,911
Islington,	North..	8,723	Chelsea	.. .. ..	12,415
„	West ..	7,451	St. George's, Hanover-sq.		10,406
			Westminster		7,925

		No. of Voters.			No. of Voters.
Islington, East	.. ..	9,022	Strand	.	11,254
„ South	.. ..	7,843	City	.. ..	31,593
Hackney, North	.. ..	8,939	Wandsworth..	..	12,014
„ Central	..	7,918	Battersea ..	.. ..	10,988
„ South	.. ..	9,078	Clapham ..	.. ..	10,020
Hammersmith	.. ..	10,326	Lambeth, North ..	..	7,870
Kensington, North	..	8,355	„ Kennington	..	9,277
„ South	..	8,805	„ Brixton ..	..	8,959
Paddington, North	.. ..	5,953	„ Norwood ..	..	7,932
„ South	.. ..	5,174	Newington, West ..	..	6,893
Marylebone, West	.. ..	8,120	„ Walworth	..	6,223
„ East	.. ..	6,956	Southwark, West ..	..	8,296
Finsbury { Central	..	7,785	„ Bermondsey	..	10,164
{ Holborn	..	11,333	„ Rotherhithe	..	8,919
„ East	.. ..	6,140	Camberwell, North	..	9,900
Shoreditch { Haggerston	..	6,441	„ Dulwich ..	..	9,280
{ Hoxton	..	8,293	„ Peckham	..	10,402
Bethnal-green, North-east	6,810		Deptford ..	..	10,473
„ South-west	7,907		Lewisham ..	..	10,193
Twr. Hmlts., Whitechapel	6,922		Greenwich ..	..	8,719
„ St. George's	3,663		Woolwich ..	..	10,893
„ Stepney	..	6,378			

It only remains to be stated that while throughout the country courts of quarter sessions are busy in dividing the various administrative counties into electoral divisions for the purposes of the Local Government Act, no such work is necessary in the metropolis, because the Act itself prescribes that every metropolitan borough shall be an electoral division, and that where a borough is divided already into divisions, each of such divisions shall have its own representation on the County Council. The elections are to take place in January, and already there are signs among the metropolitan constituencies of candidates who intend seeking the suffrages of the county electors. The lists of voters for the

metropolis have already been made out and are
in course of revision.   It will be the fault of the
county electors of the new administrative County
of London if they do not send to the council-table
a more vigorous and more independent body of
men than have recently sat on the Metropolitan
Board of Works.   The fact that the representatives are subject to popular election will certainly
render them more sensitive to popular criticism
than the gentlemen of whom some seem to have
found membership of the Metropolitan Board
both pleasant and profitable.

III.—THE ELECTION OF COUNTY COUNCILLORS.

After an experience extending over a long series of years, the inhabitants of our municipal boroughs have probably become familiarized with the mode of election to municipal office. Even they must have had their minds disturbed from time to time by the interpretation which the Courts have placed upon the Acts of Parliament governing the municipal franchise and regulating the modes of election. Perplexed, however, as the municipal voter may be, he probably has a general idea of the steps necessary to be taken to obtain a seat on his town council ; but the average candidate for the new county councils has no experience to guide him, and a perusal of the Acts of Parliament, without reference to the reported decisions of the Courts, will not help him much. The pedestrian would be puzzled by a signpost pointing in two different directions to the same place, so the candidate may be forgiven if he fails to understand some of the conflicting rules which Parliament has laid down for his direction and guidance. The Judges have done their best to reconcile conflicting enactments. but in doing so they have sometimes upset opinions which had been commonly received and acted upon for some years. While it would be impossible within any reasonable limits to give a detailed and reliable guide which should be useful to the county elector and to the county candidate in every possible emergency, there are so many well-defined pitfalls in which the unwary candidate might easily find himself that a few general hints on the subject of the candidature and nomination, and subsequently as to the election, will be useful, although not superseding recourse to a legal adviser in any unforeseen difficulty that should occur.

The first point that a candidate for the county council will have to consider will be the area over which his constituency will extend. He is to be a member of the council for his county. The Local Government Board some weeks since settled the number of county councillors for each of the county councils in England and Wales. The numbers vary from 210 for the county of York to 21 for the county of Rutland. For the purposes of the Local Government Act, York is cut up into three administrative counties. The West Riding of York will have 90 councillors, and the other Ridings 61 and 59 respectively. The largest county council, indeed, appears to be that of London, but the number for London was settled by the Local Government Act itself, and did not depend upon the discretion of the Local Government Board. The next largest is

Lancaster, the county council of which is to have 105 members. The other counties vary in number, and are generally to have between 50 and 60 members. These numbers are exclusive of the aldermen, who will be elected. But the Local Government Board have only settled the number of members to each county council; the electoral divisions have to be settled for the purposes of the first elections by the Courts of Quarter Sessions, and these bodies are now busy doing that work. It is to be completed by November 8, and as the county justices are beginning to feel that they may not after all despise a seat on the county councils, the precise constitution and boundaries of the electoral divisions have considerable interest for them. That the work of cutting up the counties into electoral divisions would be difficult in the ordinary way is sufficiently obvious, but the Local Government Act has made it more difficult by the directions that have been laid down. The populations of the electoral divisions are to be as nearly as may be equal, and regard is to be had to the proper representation of the rural and the urban population, to the distribution and pursuits of such population, and to area as well as to the last published census, and to evidence of any considerable change of population since that census. There are, moreover, a number of other detailed instructions to which it is not interesting to refer. To the candidate the constitution of the electoral division is all important. Until this question has been settled, the candidate cannot tell what towns and villages he will have to canvass, nor how many miles he may have to drive, in order effectually to stump the constituency

He will not know how many meetings he may have to address, nor how much money the Corrupt Practices Act will allow him to spend in promoting his candidature. By November 8, however, all this is to be settled ; and, indeed, before that date those intending candidates who are in the secrets of the Sessions-house will probably have a very good idea of the manner in which their own particular county will be cut up into electoral divisions.

The electoral divisions, then, having been settled and the candidate having determined to offer his services to his neighbours, he must ascertain that he is duly qualified. If his name be not on the several lists which now are being revised he may say " good-bye " at once to his chance of a seat at the county council—absence of the name from the register of voters is absolutely fatal to the would-be candidate. Whether the name has been omitted by mere negligence, or by malicious proceedings on the part of a political opponent, or by mischance matters not ; if, when the list leaves the hands of the Revising Barrister, the would-be candidate's name is not there he is absolutely precluded from coming forward unless he be a peer owning property in the county, or be registered as a Parliamentary voter in respect of the ownership of property in the county. Unfortunately, however, for the candidate, the fact that the name is on the list is not conclusive in his favour ; it must not only be there, but he must be entitled to have it there. Assuming, however, that our candidate possesses the proper qualification, and is not under any disability, and is not concerned in any contract which will be transferred from the county justices to the county council, he will, after taking such preliminary steps as may be necessary to make his candidature known, have to think about the formal requisites for his nomination. It is the opinion of the Local Government Board that ladies are not eligible for the county council. From a casual observation that was dropped by Mr. Justice A. L. Smith in a recent case it is also his opinion that women are not qualified to be members of a town council and therefore of a county council. The Municipal Corporations Act contains a clause stating that words importing the masculine gender shall include women for all purposes connected with and having reference to the right to vote at municipal elections. The inference is, therefore, quite correctly drawn, according to the accepted mode of interpreting Acts of Parliament, that for all purposes excepting the right to vote words importing masculine gender are to include men only. So, whatever may have been the intention of the Legislature, we cannot have lady county councillors, nor can we have county alderwomen. A candidate need not live within his county. A separate list is made of those who live within 15 miles of the county for which they stand, and they are just as eligible for the county council as residents in the county, nor need the candidate reside within the electoral division which he seeks to represent. As long as his name is on and entitled to be on the county register he is eligible to represent any division of the county, but he can only be nominated and supported by electors for the particular division for which he stands. The nomination requires the signature as proposer and seconder of two electors and the support of eight electors. The following is a form of nomination paper adapted from the schedule of the Municipal Corporations Act :—

B—2

COUNTY OF ———

Election of one councillor for ———— Division, in the said county, to be held on the — January, 1889.

NOMINATION PAPER.

We, the undersigned, being respectively electors for the above Division, hereby nominate the following person as a candidate at the said election :—

Surname.	Other Names.	Abode.	Description.

Signature.	Number on Register, with the Division or Polling District, if any, having a Distinct Numbering.
	——Polling District No.........
	——Polling District No.........

We, the undersigned, being respectively electors for the above division, hereby assent to the nomination of the above-named person as a candidate at the said election.

Dated this — day of January, 1889.

Here follow the signatures of eight electors, with number on the register, showing the division or polling district, if any, having a distinct numbering.

The completion of the nomination paper and its delivery involve compliance with numerous technicalities. There is a section in the Municipal Corporations Act which appears intended to provide against serious consequences follow-

ing any misdescription or misnomer. In that
section nomination papers are not referred to,
and the Courts have occasionally been very strict
in dealing with nomination papers and mistakes
made therein. At one time it appeared that
some slight licence would be allowed. In a case
in 1884 the Court of Queen's Bench thought that
" Wm." did not clearly represent the Christian
name " William," and, indeed, there had been
previous decisions which gave colour to
that view, but the Court of Appeal, while
considering that " W." might not have
been sufficient because Walter or Wilbraham
might have been meant, yet thought that "Wm.""
meant clearly William, and so allowed the paper.
The mere fact, however, that serious litigation
has occurred on a point of the kind indicates the
necessity for absolute care in all steps relating
to nomination papers. This decision of the
Court of Appeal is probably one which would
commend itself to the mind of every layman ;
but in a later case a very serious view was taken
of a variance between the name in the nomination paper and the name on the burgess roll.
More than one writer of standing had advised
that where a name appeared incorrectly on a
burgess roll, and it was desired to nominate
the person as to whose name a mistake had been
made, his correct name should be entered in the
nomination paper, together with his number on
the burgess roll, so that identification would
be easy ; but in a case which was deliberately
discussed in 1885 one Charles Arthur Burman
signed a nomination paper as an assenting burgess. His number on the burgess
roll was correctly inserted against his name. An
examination of the nomination paper, however,
by a microscopical eye discovered that the Bur-

man No. 467 on the burgess roll was there
entered as Charles Burman whereas the assenting burgess had signed his name as Charles
Arthur Burman, and the Court of Queen's Bench
was asked to declare that Charles Arthur Burman
who signed the nomination paper as No. 467 on
the burgess roll might be held to be identical
with the Charles Burman who appeared opposite
No. 467 on the burgess roll. At this, however,
the Court of Queen's Bench struck ; they considered that burgesses ought to be able to decide
whether a candidate is properly nominated and
assented to without any trouble or doubt ;
that they ought to be able to say whether the
right person had signed a nomination paper and
burgess roll without " further and laborious
inquiry," and thereupon the nomination paper
was disallowed. Upon this case, therefore, the
best advice to give candidates and their sup-
porters is that they should closely examine the
register of voters and take care that on the nomination papers the names of all who sign be so
written as to correspond to the dot of the " i " and
the cross of the "t" with the precise letter of the
name as it appears on the register of voters. This
will be the safer course to pursue, although it
may be that the tide of legal opinion will not
always roll with equally destructive force. Indeed,
there was a sign of its ebbing slightly three
months ago when the Queen's Bench Division
admitted the signatures as assenting burgesses
to the nomination of " Edwin J. Hooper," whose
name appeared as Edwin John Hooper on the burgess roll ; of " W. E. Waller," whereas the
name on the burgess roll was William
E. Waller ; and of " R. Turner," instead of
Robert Turner as it appeared on the burgess
roll. There has. however, been no hint that any-

thing short of full names and addresses corresponding with the burgess roll would be sufficient for the description of the candidate, and in a case where the name of a candidate is not correctly entered on the register of electors it would probably be well, after stating the full correct names, to add that the candidate is described on the register of voters in such and such a way. As will have been observed from the form of nomination paper, the candidate must be proposed and seconded, and then supported by eight electors. It must be borne in mind that it is the nomination that is assented to and supported by the eight electors, and, therefore, a nomination has been held by the Courts to be bad where, after the assentors had signed, the name of the nominator was altered. The assent, the Judges said, must follow the nomination and not precede it. It is not an uncommon practice in a municipal borough for a candidate to get his eight assentors to sign the paper, leaving the places of honour as proposer and seconder to be filled by persons of distinguished position, but this course is irregular, and if found out would be dangerous. The nomination paper, having been filled up, signed, and the numbers on the register of electors duly and correctly inserted, has to be delivered at the returning officer's office by the candidate in person, or by his proposer or seconder—sending by post, or parcel, or messenger will not do, there must be a personal delivery of the paper at the prescribed office.

The first elections for the county councils in England are to be held in January, and the notices of election have to be published by the returning officer in December next. The returning officer is to fix between the nomination and election a period not exceeding six days, and

as under the Act notice has to be published next
December and the election cannot take place
earlier than January 14th candidates will have
plenty of time to prepare themselves for a
personal journey to the place of nomination.
There are two apparently contradictory rules in
the Municipal Corporations Act with regard to
the number of nomination papers that an elector
may sign. One rule states that the same
burgesses may subscribe as many nomination
papers as there are vacancies to be filled, and
another rule lays it down that where a person
subscribes more nomination papers than one his
subscription is to be inoperative in all but the
one which is first delivered. The first of these
rules (Rule 3) was the expression of the law
existing at the time the Act was passed, and the
second of the rules (Rule 10) was introduced as
an amendment in Committee as the Bill was
passing through the House. The Courts have
had these two rules under their consideration,
but it may be doubted whether a satisfactory decision has been given. It has been suggested
that Rule 3 applied to an election where there
were several vacancies, and that Rule 10—the
rule which restricts the effective signature of
burgesses to one nomination paper—applied only
to such elections as those for the county council,
where (except in London) there will be only one
vacancy. It is possible, however, that these two
rules will be the subject of further litigation, and
perhaps a higher and possibly a different opinion
may be given. In the meantime, candidates would
do well to ask each elector who signs his nomination paper, whether proposer, seconder, or assen-
tor, whether he has signed any previous paper,
and, if so, it would be safest to leave that par-

ticular elector alone and to get someone else to sign in his place.

The next act in the process of nomination is the scrutiny of the nomination papers. On the day after the date fixed for delivery of nomination papers the returning officer is to attend at the place of which he shall have given notice, for a sufficient time between 2 and 4, to decide on the validity of every objection, made in writing, to the nomination papers. The candidate may attend before the returning officer himself, or he may be represented by, or have the assistance of, one person, who must be appointed in writing, and whose appointment must be delivered to the returning officer before 5 o'clock on the day fixed for delivery of nomination papers. No one, unless for the purpose of assisting the returning officer, is allowed to be present when the objections to nomination papers are dealt with, except, of course, the candidates and their duly-appointed representatives. Each candidate or his representative may object to the nomination paper of any other candidate for the same electoral division. The unsuspecting candidate might suppose that the returning officer could under these provisions deal with all sorts of objections, but here again the Courts have stopped in, and the House of Lords, this time, has very emphatically declared that the powers of the returning officer are exceedingly limited. The qualification of a candidate had been considered a matter which the returning officer could hear arguments upon and decide. It was, however, Lord Herschell said in the House of Lords, " impossible to suppose that such a question as the qualification of a candidate should, on it may be very imperfect information and without legal assistance, be finally and conclusively determined by a returning officer, who in this case was the mayor of a municipal borough." It had previously been decided that a mayor had no power to deal with an objection as to the time of the delivery of nomination papers, and therefore the candidate who is confident that the names of his proposer and seconder and also of his assentors correspond to the entries on the register of electors, and that their numbers on the register are correctly stated, need fear very little from the ordeal of the examination of the nomination paper before the returning officer. If, however, the candidate prefers not to come face to face with his opponent but feels faint-hearted and dislikes the prospect of a contest, he can at any time before 2 on the day for objection withdraw his candidature by giving notice in writing to the returning officer.

It may be convenient to intending candidates to know that their personal presence in this country at the time of nomination is not absolutely requisite if they have, in the presence of two witnesses within one month before the day of nomination, signed a consent to be a candidate, which consent has to be produced at the time the nomination paper is delivered in.

The further proceedings towards the election of a candidate will be dealt with in a separate paper, but in connexion with the candidature some very important rules laid down by the Municipal Elections Corrupt Practices Act, 1884, have to be observed. A candidate might very innocently infringe some of the provisions of that Act, and might unwittingly render himself liable, not only to the loss of his seat and to unpleasant disqualification, but even to serious punishment. The Act, of course, prohibits all corrupt practices, Treating, undue influence, and bribery hardly need in these days any detailed definition. Candidates for the county council are probably quite familiar with the prohibitions which exist in the case of Parliamentary elections against practices of this sort. Those prohibitions will apply equally to elections for the county council; but, in addition to those practices which would probably strike the ordinary candidate as being corrupt, many things innocent in themselves are, by the Act referred to, made illegal practices. First, the total sum which a candidate may spend in and about his election is limited to £25, with an additional 3d. for each elector above the first 500 electors. In a constituency numbering 5,000 electors the *maximum* amount that can be spent by any one candidate would, therefore, be £81 5s. Another provision of the Act prohibits the use of more than one committee-room for every 2,000, or any incomplete part of 2,000 electors. No committee-room may be held on any premises licensed for selling intoxicating liquor or refreshment, whether food or drink, nor on any premises where any intoxicating liquor is supplied to members of a club, society, or association, nor may a meeting for promoting the election of a candidate be held on any such premises as these. The number of persons that may be employed for payment is limited to two persons for the first 2,000 electors, and one person in addition for every 1,000 electors beyond 2,000. One polling agent may be employed in each polling station, and a person may be legally paid who is an elector, but if so employed he may not vote. Then, municipal elections are supposed to be sufficiently enlivening not to require the use of bands of music, torches, flags, banners, cockades, ribands, or other marks of distinction, and any payment or promise of payment in respect of any of these things is an illegal payment, and subjects the person paying and the person receiving to punishment. No payment may be made on account of the conveyance of electors, and it is also important to remember that no public or hackney carriage, nor any horse kept for drawing the same, nor any carriage horse or other animal which is kept or used to be let out on hire may be used for the conveyance of electors to or from the poll. It matters not whether the use of the horse is paid for or not, if it be a horse that is kept for being let out for hire it may not be used even gratuitously at the election. An elector may himself take a cab, or two or three electors may combine to pay for one for themselves. Another point to be borne in mind by the candidate is that every bill, placard, or poster, and, to be safe, every circular or card having reference to the election must bear upon it the name and address of the printer and publisher. If it does not, the candidate, if he have printed or published, or caused it to be printed or published, is guilty of an illegal practice, his election may be declared void, he may be fined £100, and will be incapable for five years of voting at any election. It is also necessary for the candidate to remember that every claim made against him in respect of the election expenses must be sent in within 14 days of the date of election, and if not sent in within that time will be barred. All the expenses that he has incurred must be paid within 21 days, and within 28 days he is to make a return of his expenses to the returning officer.

The points which have been referred to are those which it is most necessary for a candidate to keep in mind during his candidature, and if the mere enumeration of some of the provisions of the Act should have startled a timid candidate, he may be reassured when he learns that the High Court of Justice has power to excuse an innocent offender from the consequence of some indiscretion or inadvertence if only the Court be satisfied of his *bona fides*, and if he apply promptly after the discovery of his mistake. When the Act was first passed the Judges were very indulgent, they have been gradually getting more and more strict. No doubt, however, the first candidates for the county councils will receive merciful consideration for any mistakes that they may make, if only it appears to the Court that the mistakes arose from ignorance of the provisions of the statute or real inadvertence. If, however, the act committed were one which in any way had helped a candidate to success at his election the Court would be very loth and very unlikely to excuse it.

IV.—THE COUNTY COUNCILLORS—THEIR ELECTION AND FIRST MEETINGS.

It is, of course, the returning officer who will provide the election machinery ; the place for taking the poll and for counting the votes will be appointed by him. He also will provide presiding officers, poll clerks, ballot papers, and everything that is necessary to ascertain the opinions of the electors. The returning officer for the first elections will be the sheriff of the county, unless, indeed, he should be desirous of becoming a candidate, and then he may apply to quarter sessions, and quarter sessions may appoint some one to act as returning officer for the first elections. In the county of London the appointment of returning officer for the first election is vested in the Local Government Board. The first returning officer will have considerable power, for it devolves upon him to divide the electoral divisions into polling districts. He is to take care that every polling district shall be the area or a combination of areas for which separate parts of the register of electors are made out, but subject to that he appears to have entire discretion over the constitution of polling districts. This, as everyone who has any experience in connexion with elections must know, is a very important function, the discharge of which may materially affect the exercise of the franchise. It may, indeed, in some cases practically shut out from voting a number of electors if the polling districts be improperly constituted. The candidate can, if he please, amuse himself from 8 a.m. to 8 p.m. by driving round and visiting such of the polling stations as are within reach. He may also have present in each station, if he so desire it, an agent, who must have previously been appointed by the candidate, and who must have made a declaration that he will observe secrecy, and will not disclose information as to who has or who has not voted. The agent is generally to aid in maintaining the secrecy of the ballot proceedings. The appointment of the agent has to be notified to the returning officer one clear day before the polling day, and it must be borne in mind that if an elector accepts for payment the appointment of polling agent he will not be entitled to vote at the election.

On the mode of voting much might be said. Numerous decisions of the Courts have been recorded allowing and disallowing ballot papers marked in all sorts of fantastic ways. Without referring to reported cases in detail, it may suffice for candidates to remember that the helpless or illiterate voter is entitled to every possible assistance at the hands of the presiding officer. The stupid and blundering voter may misunderstand the directions as to filling up his ballot paper, but if he succeeds in putting anything on it which will indicate the way in which he desires to vote without at the same time being likely to cause his identification the vote will be recorded. If, for instance, he puts a dash instead of a cross in the space which the voter has to mark, the dash will be allowed ; but if he puts his initials instead of a cross the vote will be dis-

allowed. Mistakes on the part of the voter the candidate must take his chance of, and be comforted by remembering that mistakes are just as likely to be made by those who wish to vote for his opponents as by those who desire to vote for himself. In the process of voting electors must not be interfered with, and, indeed, nowadays it is dangerous to interfere with them outside the polling station. The employment of men " to keep the boys away and to distribute handbills outside the polling stations " was severely commented upon in the Stepney case. Apart from any other circumstance, such an employment of men is not one of those things contemplated by the Corrupt Practices Act, if allowed by it. Other considerations are, moreover, provoked, and Judges have thrown out a hint that under some circumstances the employment of men sufficiently burly " to keep the boys away " might possibly amount to intimidation of voters. If gratuitous labour can be employed for the distribution, the nature of the handbill will have to be considered. It had not been uncommon to print cards showing a sort of facsimile of the ballot paper, but with one candidate's name in very large type and the others' in very small letters, and with a cross against the name of the favourite candidate. Then a note would be put at the foot of the card stating that, if the ballot paper were marked in any other way than that intimated above, the vote would be lost. It seems tolerably clear from what has dropped from various members of election courts that such cards would be condemned as fraudulent devices, and might, therefore, invalidate an election. Handbills saying :—
" Vote for Jones and Economy " or " Vote for Smith and Efficiency " would be permissible if distributed without necessitating the employment

of unauthorized agents and without obstructing or intimidating voters.

After the clock has struck 8 in the evening no more ballot papers are to be given out. There may be persons in the room waiting to vote, but they will not be entitled to receive a paper, and they must be consoled for the loss of the franchise by a reminder that they should have attended earlier in the day. As soon as the last paper delivered out before 8 has been filled up and placed in the ballot box, the ballot box will be sealed to be taken off to the place of counting the votes. During this process the candidate and agents are entitled to be present. These agents must also have been appointed beforehand, and must have made their declarations of secrecy. They will not be allowed to interfere with the counting, but an opportunity must be afforded them by the returning officer of seeing how it is done. In all probability the returning officer will be very happy to afford them every facility for checking the counting, and, indeed, will be glad that someone should control the figures ascertained by his own staff. Precautions are provided against the insertion of a number of forged ballot papers into the ballot boxes. Not only does the presiding officer have to see that the official mark is on the papers put into the ballot box, but before the votes are dealt with the first duty enjoined on the returning officer is that the papers taken from each box should be counted and compared with a statement, which the presiding officer will have handed in, showing the number of papers which he has issued at his polling station and the number of blank papers and counterfoils which he has returned. This having been done, the papers are to be mixed, so that it shall not be seen what proportion of votes for a particular candidate may come from any special district, and then the counting will proceed. The doubtful papers will be adjudicated upon by the returning officer and the result declared.

Within 10 days of the date of election the candidate has to sign a declaration that he takes upon himself the office of councillor, and within 21 days he must pay every expense that he has incurred. If he make a single payment after the expiration of 21 days the payment will be an illegal one and entail liability to the consequences referred to in the last paper on this subject. There is, however, a provision giving power to the High Court of Justice or to a County Court, in the case of a council election, to allow a claim to be sent in and expenses to be paid after the time limited. The accounts having been sent in and paid, a return, vouched by bills stating the particulars and accompanied by receipts, has to be verified by a statutory declaration, and within 28 days after the day of election handed over to the returning officer. The returning officer keeps the statement of accounts and declaration for 12 months, and is bound to show them to anyone on payment of 1s., and to deliver copies on payment of a small prescribed fee. While cases have occurred in which the Courts have exercised their power of excuse, and have given absolution to candidates who have failed to comply with these provisions, yet there have been cases in which the absolution has been refused, and no candidate can safely make a payment without permission of the Court after 21 days of the date of election, nor can he safely omit after 28 days to send in his return. The particulars of expenditure given must be sufficient to enable the different expenses incurred to be identified and, if need be, to be complained of. If, for instance, it appears that the travelling expenses of an elector have been paid, and an entry is made in the account to that effect, the election may be upset; so, too, where it appeared that persons had been employed to keep order at a meeting connected with an election. That was held to be an illegal employment, as were also refresh ments given to people who had been called " workers " at an election. On the other hand, the candidate who has by accident made an illegal payment cannot safely omit it from his return, for then he will be liable to serious punishment. He must, therefore, make the best of it, and take the consequences.

The Act requiring a return of expenses and declaration applies equally in cases where no expenses at all have been incurred. This was held in a recent case, and the Queen's Bench Division were very emphatic in laying down the law that, notwithstanding a candidate had incurred no expenses at all, he must make the declaration in the prescribed form ; for one object of that declaration is to negative the expenditure of money by other persons on behalf of the candidate.

Our candidate may have thought it desirable to have two strings to his bow and to stand for two electoral divisions. If this should have been the case, and if he has been lucky enough to be elected in both, he must declare in writing to the returning officer his choice of the division for which he will sit ; and if he should not be able to make up his mind, then the returning officer is to make the choice for him before the first meeting of the provisional council. It is not intended by the Act that one county councillor shall at the same time represent two electoral divisions.

The candidate having been duly elected will not enter upon his duties as a fully-fledged councillor until the 1st of April, or such other day as the Local Government Board may appoint, but on the second Thursday next after the day fixed for the first election the county councillors will hold a meeting as a provisional council. Of that meeting notice will be given by the returning officer at the same time that he sends the councillor formal intimation of his election, and the hour and place of meeting will be determined by the returning officer. At this meeting the provisional councillors will elect one of their number to be chairman of that and of the second meeting, and they will then proceed to elect the county aldermen. Now these aldermen may or may not have been elected members of the council, but if not councillors they must be persons who would have been qualified to be on the council. They are to be elected according to the provisions of the Municipal Corporations Act and with the formalities prescribed by that statute. The mode of election is by every councillor entitled to vote delivering at the meeting to the chairman a voting paper containing the surname and other names, the place of abode, and description of the person for whom he votes. This enactment must be strictly complied with. Voting papers which contained the description of the place where the candidate daily transacted his business instead of his place of abode were held to be bad, although the description was made without fraud or intention to mislead, and was such as would be commonly understood to apply to the person voted for. In another case the benevolent intention of the section of the Act intended to prevent the occurrence of injustice by accidental misnomer was much cramped by the Court. A candidate a few days prior to his election had removed from Gonville-road to Newmarket-road, but in his voting paper he was described as of Gonville-road, and the Judges considered that "this was not an inaccurate description of a place," but was an "accurate description of a wrong place" and not covered by the statute. In another case the name, surname, and place of abode of the candidate were given, but he was not described, and the vote was thrown out. These instances are selected from several to show the absolute necessity for the utmost care in filling up voting papers in the election of aldermen. The voting paper has to be signed. There is no secrecy about it, and, indeed, as soon as all the voting papers have been given to the chairman he has openly to produce and read them or cause them to be read. Any would-be alderman should therefore take care, unless it be beneath his dignity to do so, that the councillors who intend to vote for him are furnished with accurate particulars as to his surname and other names, place of abode, and description. At the same meeting the county councillors are to determine by ballot which of the aldermen shall serve for three years only, and which for six, for under the provisions of the Act one-half of the aldermen first elected, will have to retire at the end of three years' service. In many cases, however, the number of aldermen is not divisible by two, and then the larger half are to retire first at the end of three years, and the lesser half will remain in office for six years.

If the county councillors should be unable to choose the aldermen, or should they discuss the election of chairman at such length as to give

them no time for the process of electing aldermen, they may adjourn their first meeting, and
at the adjourned meeting elect the aldermen, but
they appear to have no power to transact any
other business at the first meeting. At the
second meeting of the provisional council the
county aldermen are to be summoned to attend,
and at that meeting or at the adjournment thereof the chairman and vice-chairman of the county
council may be chosen.

Of course, if county councillors have been elected
aldermen, vacancies will have been caused on the
council, and it would probably be a compliance
with the spirit, although not necessarily according to the letter, of the Act for the second meeting to be held at such time as would permit of
the vacancies having been filled up and of the
full provisional council being present. As the
quorum necessary for the transaction of business at the ordinary council meeting is one-fourth
of the whole number, so it is presumed that the
same proportion of members of the provisional
council will be competent to transact the preliminary business which is contemplated.

The chairman of the first and second meetings
of the provisional county council is to have a
second or casting vote in case of equality of
votes, and where on the selection of the chairman an equal number of votes is given to two or
more persons, the meeting is to determine by lot
which of those persons shall be the chairman.

The term of office of chairman will apparently
be regulated by the provisions of the Municipal
Corporations Act which make the mayor an
annual officer. Under the Municipal Corporations
Act the mayor is not necessarily a member of the
council, but he must possess the qualifications
necessary for a councillor ; so it would appear

that the chairman of the county council may be like the mayor of a borough, " a fit person elected by the council from among the aldermen or councillors or persons qualified to be such." It would appear, too, by the incorporation of the Municipal Corporations Act, that the chairman of a county council may, like the mayor, receive " such remuneration as the council think reasonable."

In London a deputy chairman may be chosen, and the county council may pay him such remuneration as they may from time to time think fit. It will be remembered that the chairman of the Metropolitan Board of Works receives a salary, and the option of appointing a deputy chairman with remuneration is doubtless to enable the county council of London, which will be the most important county council in the kingdom, to secure the services of a second person of distinction and ability, who will hold a higher rank than that of clerk to the council, but upon whose services the council may be entitled to rely. The deputy chairman will probably be chairman of the finance committee, or a sort of metropolitan Chancellor of the Exchequer.

The business of the provisional council, the aldermen and chairman having been elected, is to provide for bringing the provisions of the Act into full operation on the appointed day, and to make the necessary arrangements with quarter sessions, and to provide for all such matters as are necessary to enable the county council, as now fully constituted, to execute its duties and to give full effect to the Act. The provisional council will be entitled to use the county buildings, and the clerk of the peace and his officers and the quarter sessions officers are, if required, to act

as officers of the provisional council ; but. on
the other hand, the provisional council may hire
buildings and appoint interim officers, and pay
them as it may think fit to do so.   The proceedings for filling up the casual vacancies caused on
the council by the election of any councillors to
the office of alderman will be similar to those prescribed for the first election.   The sheriff or other
person who acted as returning officer at the first
election will be returning officer in respect of the
casual vacancies, and the new councillor appointed will hold his office for the term during
which the person whom he succeeds would have
acted.

The term of office of the councillors is three
years.   They are then all to retire together, and
their places are to be filled by a new election, and
the county councillors first elected are to retire
from office on the ordinary day of the election in
the third year after the passing of the Act—viz.,
1891.   On the 7th of November in the same year
the retiring aldermen will either be re-elected or
their places will be filled up.   The triennial re-
tirement of all the councillors is a variation from
the practice in municipal boroughs, where one-
third only of the council retire every year.   Thus
something like continuity of policy is secured.
The aldermanic element in the county councils is
supposed to be the element of stability.   As half
the aldermen retire in the year in which there
may be a clean sweep of the council chamber, the
stability of the council will depend upon a leaven
consisting of one-eighth in number of the whole
council—a very little leaven to leaven the whole
lump.

V.—THE COUNTY COUNCILLORS AT WORK.

The county councillor will search the Local Government Act in vain for any complete code of regulations as to the conduct of the council business. The directions which have to be followed are dotted about in the Local Government Act and in the Municipal Corporations Act. The second schedule to the latter Act contains an approach to something like a code which the county councillor should learn by heart, and which has all the advantage of antiquity. Most of the rules contained in this second schedule were reproduced verbatim from the Act which reformed the municipal corporations in 1835. Many of them had been in force for many years before that date. It would, however, have been very convenient if in a schedule to the Local Government Act the county councillor could have found collected in a few paragraphs all the rules which will have to be followed. This, however, is not to be found, and a brief sketch may therefore be given here which will perhaps prove of some service.

If the number of necessary meetings be taken as a criterion, Parliament has not contemplated that the county councils should be over-worked. There need only be four meetings in the course

of the year. One of these is to be held at noon
on the 7th of November, and the three other statutory meetings are to be held on such dates as the
councils may on the 7th of November, or by standing order, appoint. With the exception of the
7th of November meeting, at which the chairman
is to be elected, and at which every three years
aldermen are to be appointed, the meetings can
be held at such time as may be fixed ; and as to
all the meetings, there is no necessity to hold
them within the limits of the county itself.
The chairman may at any time call a meeting of
the council and any five members may require the chairman to convene one. If he
should refuse, or if he should fail after
the prescribed time to obey a requisition of this
sort, the five members may themselves summon
their colleagues together. Apart from this pro-
cedure the council can, of course, appoint as many
meetings as they think fit. The county council of
London, succeeding to the powers and duties of
the Metropolitan Board of Works, would find it
impossible to transact all its business in four
quarterly meetings, and that particular council
will probably find it desirable to meet weekly, or
at least fortnightly. In many of the counties of
England the distances which will have to be
traversed by members of the council will probably incline them to follow in the footsteps of
their predecessors, the Courts of Quarter Sessions,
and to hold four meetings only in the year. The
experience of the town councils of our municipal
boroughs will hardly give a lead in this respect
to the county councils, for the districts governed
by the municipal corporations are compact, and
attendance at the council meetings seldom involves
any long journeyings. But in many of the smaller
boroughs the town councils confine themselves

to quarterly meetings, while in the larger boroughs monthly meetings are generally the rule, although in exceptional cases the councils meet fortnightly. The council meetings will be presided over by the chairman, and in his absence at the time of holding the meeting the councillors present must elect one of their number to preside. Although they have power to elect a vice-chairman at the same time that they choose their chairman, yet the vice-chairman is not entitled to preside at any council meeting unless specially elected at the time to the chair. Parliament has provided against meetings being held without proper notice to the councillors, and in a borough notice of an intended meeting has to be fixed on the town-hall, but in a county it will have to be fixed " in some conspicuous place." This notice, in the case of a meeting called upon a requisition of members, has to specify the business to be done at the meeting, but in other cases it will merely state the time and place at which the meeting is to be held. As, however, it is obvious that a notice of this kind is very likely to escape the attention of members of the council it is further provided that three clear days before any meeting is held a summons stating the business to be transacted is either to be delivered or sent by registered letter to every member of the council at his place of abode. The summons will state pretty fully what business is to be dealt with. The Local Government Act makes a special provision for the protection and guidance of the inexperienced bodies which it creates, and directs that if any resolution for paying a sum exceeding £50 out of the County Fund, or for incurring any cost, debt, or liability exceeding that sum, is to be proposed. the_notice of meeting shall state

the amount and the purpose for which the money
is required.

This is a truly paternal provision, and one which
it will be somewhat difficult to carry out, considering that the annual expenditure of some of the
county councils will exceed a quarter of a million,
and that in comparatively few cases will it be less
than £30,000. It is also rather singular, but it
is the fact, that certain business to be transacted
at the quarterly meetings need not be specified
in the summons. In giving notice for the meeting of the 7th of November it would be considered
" bad form " on the part of the clerk of the
peace, but it would be quite legal, to omit from
the summons such items as the election of chairman and the election of aldermen, and so the unwary councillor might possibly be induced, by
press of his own business or other circumstances,
to neglect attending a meeting at which business
certainly of interest and probably of importance
would be transacted. But such a contingency is
hardly likely to arise, and the councillor will
himself be to blame if he should forget that on
the 7th of November, all over England and Wales,
chairmen, and every three years aldermen, are to
be elected.

The acts of the council and all questions arising
before it are to be decided by a majority of
the members present and voting, and in case
of equality of votes the chairman has a second or
casting vote. The minutes of the meeting need
not be written while the meeting is proceeding,
and if not signed at the time they may be signed
at the next ensuing meeting by the chairman
himself or by some member of the council de-
scribing himself as chairman of the meeting at
which the minute is signed.

The minutes are open to the inspection of any

county elector on payment of 1s., and he may copy or take extracts from them. It is, of course, impossible that all business of the class that will have to be transacted by county councils can be done by the full council in regular meeting assembled, and so they have power to appoint committees, and particularly they are required to appoint a finance committee, without whose recommendation a payment cannot be made. Moreover, they will have to join with the Court of Quarter Sessions in appointing a joint committee, who will have power to appoint and remove the clerk of the peace. It has already been stated that the existing clerks of the peace are to be clerks of the county councils, but it is an error to suppose that future clerks of the peace can be appointed by county councils; they can only be appointed, and they can be removed, by the joint committee, and the joint committee may appoint a deputy clerk to act in lieu of the clerk, in case of death, illness, or absence from any other cause, as may be determined by the joint committee. It would seem, therefore, that, while clerks of the peace will probably retain their power to appoint deputy clerks for the purpose of judicial business, the appointment of deputy for the purposes of the Local Government Act can only be effected by the joint committee. The joint committee will also have charge of the police and the provision of accommodation for Quarter Sessions and other matters of detail. The joint committees are to consist of such equal number of Quarter Sessions justices and members of the county council as may be arranged between the Quarter Sessions and the council, or in default of arrangement as may be directed by the Secretary of State. As this constitution of the joint committee may lead to equality of voting, they are to elect a chairman. In case of equality of votes for two or more persons for the chair one of them is to be elected by lot ; thus, if the members of the joint committee appointed by Quarter Sessions and the representatives of the county councils vote together so that important questions may depend upon the casting vote of the chairman, the Act of Parliament deliberately leaves those important questions to an officer chosen by lot.

The proceedings of all the committees of the county council have to be reported to the council from time to time. This will doubtless be done in the same form that has for many years prevailed with regard to the committees of Quarter Sessions. A few days before the Quarter Sessions are held printed reports of the committees are circulated among the justices, who are thus, if they take the trouble to read their reports, fully conversant with the recommendations and business that may be brought before them. This plan is also adopted in all well regulated municipal boroughs, and is, indeed, the only way in which the council can keep its hand upon the reins.

The proceedings of the joint committee do not require any confirmation by the county council, and the county council, on the other hand, are to provide such funds as the joint committee may need in connexion with the powers which they exercise. Standing orders may be made by the county councils for the regulation of their business, and, indeed, will be necessary. It will be advisable to provide for the deliberative business being conducted with due dignity and in proper form. The number of times that any member of the council may be entitled to speak on any given subject, the nature of amendments that may be allowed, the mode of giving notice of motion, the manner of dealing with and voting upon the " previous question " should all be provided for by standing order. Besides these matters, standing orders will be wanted for regulating the proceedings as to licensing stage plays and music and dancing, but on all these points the county councillors will find any number of precedents in the municipal boroughs of standing and experience.

An interesting question may sometimes arise as to the disqualification of members of the council. One who becomes bankrupt, or compounds with his creditors, or, except in case of illness, is continuously absent from the county for more than six months, becomes disqualified. If chairman, he may only be absent two months without becoming disqualified. In case of bankruptcy or composition with his creditors, the disqualification as regards subsequent elections ceases on obtaining an order of discharge, or, in case of compounding, on payment of the debts in full. There are other disqualifying circumstances. One is accepting any office or place of profit in the gift or disposal of the council, and another is having directly or indirectly by himself or partner any share or interest in any contract or employment with, by, or on behalf of the council ; but this does not apply to a lease, sale, or purchase of land, to an agreement for the loan of money, nor to an interest in a newspaper in which the council's advertisements are inserted. So, too, a councillor may be a shareholder in a company which contracts with the council, but he must not vote or take part in the discussion of any matter in which the company or he himself have directly or indirectly any pecuniary interest.

When the county councillors take up their office their first duty will probably be to consider how far their staff is efficient for the work that will have to be done. They are to have the assistance of all the Quarter Sessions officers, including the surveyor and treasurer, and if they find it necessary to dispense with any of them they will have to pay them compensation ; but beyond the existing staff the Municipal Corporations Act gives the council ample powers to appoint such officers as it may think necessary for carrying on its duties ; the clerk of the peace and his deputy being the only officers with whose appointment the county council cannot deal. They may appoint a secretary, solicitor, or any number of clerks. A medical officer of health may be appointed, in addition to the existing staff, and his services may by arrangement be made available for any district within the county. As to his salary, and as to the pay of all the other officers, the discretion of the county council is entirely unlimited ; but it may be that the county councils will pause before they make many new appointments, and that they will devote themselves in the first instance to the consideration of the important question of finance.

To this too much attention cannot be paid. The financial operations of the counties have been of considerable magnitude. According to the last published local taxation returns the outstanding county loans amounted to upwards of three-and-a-half millions, and the annual rates levied by the counties exceeded two millions, while other items brought up their total receipts to upwards of three millions in the year. Of course, in a case like this, striking an average would not convey an accurate idea of the financial operations of the counties generally. A few

counties may be picked out by way of example.
The current receipts of Lancaster in one year
are returned at £391,524 ; Chester, Kent, Middlesex, Stafford, and Surrey are between £100,000
and £200,000 each. Of the smaller counties the
annual current receipts of Rutland are £4,095,
and those of Radnor £4,591. These last, however, are of course exceptional figures. The indebtedness has for the most part been incurred
in respect of the erection of lunatic asylums.
These buildings, with the land on which they
stand, figure for a total of £2,800,000 of the
county indebtedness, and nearly half a million
is attributable to police stations and gaols.
Not only do the total figures applicable to each
county vary somewhat in proportion to the size,
population, and wealth of the counties, but the
amounts of the rates levied in various counties
differ considerably. The highest county rate
shown in the local taxation returns is 6d. in the
pound, that being the rate levied in Mont-
gomeryshire. Herefordshire comes near to that
figure with 5¾d., and Bedfordshire with 5d.
The lowest rate levied is that in Lancashire,
which is 1 1-16d. To this the metropolitan
counties approximate very closely. The police
rate, too, varies considerably, the highest being
3¼d. and the lowest 0¾d.

As the financial circumstances of all the counties in England and Wales differ considerably,
it would not answer any useful end to offer more
than general observations with regard to the
effect that the Local Government Act may have
upon county finance. The following table shows
in a compact form the duties that are to be
transferred from the Imperial Exchequer in aid
of the rates. Subjoined to that table are the
figures of the Government grants which will be

withdrawn. It will be seen that there is a net
balance of about three millions per annum which,
in one form or another, will go to reduce local
taxation :—

GRANTS IN AID OF LOCAL TAXATION IN ENGLAND AND WALES TO BE DISCONTINUED.

	Amounts Paid in 1886-7.
Disturnpiked and main roads	£237,123
Teachers in Poor Law schools	37,318
Poor Law medical officers	147,001
Medical officers of health and inspectors of nuisances	71,939
Registrars of births and deaths	9,534
Criminal prosecutions	162,011
Pauper lunatics	479,815
Police (metropolitan, county, and borough)	1,411,833
Grants to School Boards (under 33 and 34 Vic., c. 5, s. 97)...	6,200
Awards to public vaccinators (under 30 and 31 Vic., c. 84, s. 5)...	19,000
Total	£2,582,434

LICENCE DUTIES AND OTHER IMPERIAL REVENUE TO BE RECEIVED BY THE COUNTY COUNCILS.

Duties to be transferred to the County Councils :—		Net produce in 1886-7.
Intoxicating liquor licences ...		£1,372,243
Licences to deal in game ...		5,900
Other Licence Duties :—		
Beer dealers	29,755	
Spirit dealers	103,060	
Sweet dealers	315	
Wine dealers	43,002	
Refreshment-house keepers ...	6,759	
Tobacco dealers	63,541	
Carriages or other vehicles ...	492,779	
Armorial bearings	69,184	
Male servants	123,500	
Dogs	317,241	
Game (licences to kill) ...	159,628	
Guns	68,448	
		£1,457,212
Carried forward ...		£2,835,355

Brought forward		£2,835,355
Other Licence Duties, continued :—		
Appraisers, auctioneers, and house agents...	65,655	
Pawnbrokers	28,905	
Plate dealers	39,958	
		134,518
Estimated yield of new licence duties as proposed to be modified		726,000
Estimated amount of 40 per cent. of probate duty ...		1,800,000
Total		£5,495,873

For the present neither the counties nor any of the local authorities will be troubled with the collection of the money that is to aid them in reducing their rates. The licences, probate duty, and the new horse and wheel tax, if it should be passed, will all be collected by the officers of the Inland Revenue as hitherto. Apportionments will be made by the Local Government Board, in conjunction with the Treasury, and all that the local authorities will have to do practically will be to shut their eyes, open their mouths, and swallow the plum that the Local Government Board will insert. It is not possible at present to say precisely what effect the transfer of the licence duties and the probate duty will have upon the rates of a particular district. There have to be adjustments of a somewhat complicated kind between the county finances and the finances of the municipal boroughs in the geographical counties. None of the larger boroughs, which have for the purposes of the Act been created county boroughs, will in future be liable to pay county rates. Many of those which have been quarter sessions boroughs have already enjoyed such exemption.

but those which have not been exempt will have to redeem their freedom. The provisions of the Act have been carefully framed to guard against any undue transfer of liability from counties to boroughs, or *vice versá*. It is probable that the good sense of the municipal authorities and of the new county councils will lead to agreements being made in the great majority of cases that will fairly regulate the adjustment of liabilities and assets upon the severance of the old partnerships, but if no agreement should be come to, Commissioners have been appointed who will arbitrate between the disputing authorities.

It will be interesting to see how the general scheme will work out as to its financial results. It is impossible, dealing with a large subject and with ever-varying circumstances, to lay down any general rules that shall work no hardship and that shall operate with uniform effect throughout the country. It may be, and indeed it is obvious from the estimates which the Local Government Board have prepared, that in some places the relief of local taxation will be greater than in others. The Lancashire boroughs were in a continual state of agitation while the Local Government Act was passing as to what would be the effect upon them in regard to the maintenance of their main roads, and in some of those boroughs the operation of the Act is not by any means looked upon with unmitigated satisfaction. But the British ratepayer must look upon the matter philosophically, and be content to remember that, upon the whole, £3,000,000 less per annum will have to be abstracted from his pocket in the future than has been drawn from him in the past. The county rates will in future be made and levied by the county councils. For capital expenditure they have power to borrow. The reign of decentralization which it was supposed would set in when the Local Government Bill passed is strangely inaugurated by the control of the Local Government Board over borrowing powers being extended to loans contracted by county councils. The county justices have been free from the supervision of the Local Government Board in this respect, but the county councils will not be able to borrow £5 without the sanction of the central authority. The borrowing powers are limited in that the loans they raise will have to be repaid within a period of 30 years, and the amount which, without a special provisional order, cannot be exceeded in any county is limited to one-tenth of the rateable value. That this limit is adequate appears clearly from the fact that the annual rateable value of the counties in England is £130,000,000, whereas the outstanding loans are only about one-fortieth of that sum. So that if every county should quadruple its present capital expenditure the limit would only then be reached. The county councils are directed to make up and publish an annual budget at the commencement of the financial year, and their accounts are to be audited by district auditors appointed under the Local Government Board, whose audit is to extend to the accounts of the committees appointed, whether for lunatic asylums or for the other purposes of the county councils. This audit will not, in all probability, supersede the necessity for a careful supervision of the accounts of each county council on the part of professional accountants, for it is well known that the audit of the district auditors extends rather to the legality of the payments charged in the accounts than to the general accuracy and honesty of the accounting officers.

Too much attention cannot be given by the members of the county councils to all questions of county finance. The figures with which the county councils have to deal are for the most part of considerable amount. Readjustment of the loans may in many cases cause considerable relief to the ratepayers of the present generation, whilst carefully watching balances, guarding against too much money lying idle in the hands of the county treasurers, and seeing that the best advantage is obtained in the shape of discounts for ready money payments will effect a sensible economy. This will amply repay the expenditure of a little time and will reward the application of the commercial knowledge of the merchant or banker. There will be on the county councils many members whose daily experience has qualified them to look after the pence, but though this be done the pounds will not take care of themselves, and it may be hoped that there will be on the councils a sufficiency of men whose own large business transactions will qualify them to supervise business transactions of considerable magnitude.

VI.—THE COUNTY COUNCILLORS, THEIR MINISTERIAL AND QUASI-JUDICIAL DUTIES.

Of all the Ministerial duties that will devolve upon county councillors none will make a greater demand upon their time, their patience, and their good feeling than the care of the pauper lunatic asylums. The number of patients provided for on January 1 last was 50,180. The county councillors have to see that sufficient asylums are provided for the pauper lunatics of their county, including, of course, the smaller boroughs. Even in the first instance the county councils may find themselves called upon to provide more accommodation than at present exists, for some of the courts of quarter sessions have staved off projected increases in their buildings until their successors should come into power. The county councils will have to appoint committees of visitors, who will exercise functions analogous to those of the directors of a large hotel, but more troublesome and more responsible. Happily for them they will not have to decide upon any vexed question of sanity or madness. The Act expressly excludes from their jurisdiction all power of admission or detention, but, short of that, the visitors appointed by the county council will have thrown upon them the entire responsibility of controlling large establishments which contain from 100 to upwards of 2,000 patients. They, in fact, will exercise supreme domestic authority, and it will be to the committees of visitors that the public will look for an explanation of all those mysterious cases of broken ribs, scalding in baths, and suicide which disfigure the reports made to the Commissioners of Lunacy. The expense of maintaining the patients is borne by the guardians of the unions to which the patients are chargeable. In many cases, however, the chargeable union cannot be found, and in those and some other instances the cost of board and clothing falls upon the county fund. The average cost of maintenance of patients in county and borough asylums during last year was 8s. 9d. per head per week. There has been hitherto a Treasury contribution of 4s. per week, and the figure quoted does not include the cost of providing and repairing the asylums and the necessary furniture. This, as a rule, is borne out of the county fund. But it will be seen that to maintain a large body of lunatics, many of whom are in delicate health, within the figure mentioned must require economy on the part of the visitors and a zealous co-operation on the part of the asylum superintendents. As may be expected the Act contains elaborate provisions as to joint asylums, and as to adjustments which will have to be made in the case of boroughs which have henceforward to look after their own lunatics, but who have taken their part in providing existing asylums. All these matters will be differently dealt with according to the circumstances of each particular case. Every county council will have a greater or less number of lunatics to provide for, and will have to ask some of its members to undertake the difficult, sometimes painful and often thankless, task of serving on the committee of visitors, not the least painful, but the most necessary, of whose duties is the regular inspection of the wards. Not less than two members of the committee are to do this every two months, and to see and examine as far as possible every lunatic in the asylum. The duty next in importance in point of interest and responsibility is probably that connected with reformatory and industrial schools. The care of these schools remains to the local authorities as their own surviving duty in the provision of quasi-penal accommodation. When the Prisons Act of 1877 transferred the prisons to the Government it left the charge of reformatory and industrial schools in the hands of local authorities, and now that charge is to devolve upon the county councils. The charge is no slight one. At the beginning of the present year there were under detention in the industrial schools of the country 13,388 boys and 4,096 girls, while in the reformatory schools there were 5,180 boys and 947 girls. The county councils will have to see that sufficient reformatory or industrial school accommodation is available, and they may either provide and maintain schools on their own account or contribute towards schools otherwise provided, and which are duly certified by an inspector appointed by the Home Secretary. Judged by the financial contributions which the counties have hitherto been called upon to make the subject will not be one of absorbing financial interest to the county councils, but the importance of the work done, or expected to be done, in the schools will supply the thoughtful and far-seeing councillor with a motive which, as far as his pocket is concerned, will be wanting. To the reformatory schools the county rates last year contributed £14,000 and the borough rates £9,000.

There was a Treasury allowance of £80,000 and
the profit realized on the industrial department
was £13,000, while the parents contributed
£4,800. To the industrial schools the county
rates contributed £28,000, the borough rates
£11,000, the School Boards £65,000, the Treasury
£180,000, and the children's parents £15,000,
while the industrial department left a clear
profit of £24,000. A question of considerable
interest arises as to the results attained after a
stay in these schools, and the last report of the
Home Office inspector gives interesting details
on this question. During last year 1,492
children were discharged from reformatory
schools. Of these 606 went to employment or
service, 516 were placed with their relations, 121
emigrated, 156 went to sea, 36 enlisted, 29 were
discharged from disease, and only 28 were discharged as incorrigible. From the industrial
schools 3,883 were discharged. Of these 1,768
went to employment or service, 1,231 were placed
out through their friends, 153 emigrated,
499 went to sea, 109 enlisted, 84 were discharged
as diseased, and 39 were committed to reforma-
tories. The family circumstances of the children
in the reformatory schools is not given by the
inspector, but of those in the industrial schools
details are given, and it appears that of 4,031
children only 188 had lost both parents, 229 had
been deserted by both parents, 244 were illegiti-
mate, and 1,723 of them had both parents alive
and able to take care of their children.

From the subject of reformatory and industrial
schools the mind readily turns to the question
of police. The police forces are to be under the
control of a joint committee appointed by quarter
sessions and the county councils. Although
this joint control and responsibility is provided

for, the chief constable and men under him are to
obey the lawful orders given by justices as conservators of the peace. While, moreover, the joint
committee have the management of the police
force they will not be allowed to neglect it nor to
permit it to degenerate. Hitherto a spur to
efficiency has been afforded by the grant made
out of the public funds upon the certificate of the
inspectors of constabulary. As this and all
similar grants are to cease, and the local authorities will have nothing to expect in this respect,
they are to be under a fine which will be
recoverable if the Secretary of State withholds a
certificate that the police has been maintained in
a state of efficiency both in point of numbers and
discipline. The fine is to be equivalent to half
the cost of the pay and clothing of police of
the county during the year. It is possible to
conceive that the provisions as to the police may
not at all times work quite satisfactorily to the
county councils. They will have to provide the
county fund, and if a fine be imposed they will
have to make up the deficiency by means of rates.
Yet it is quite possible that the liability to the
fine may be incurred entirely by the members of
quarter sessions outvoting on the joint committee
their colleagues who come from the county council,
and so the county council may have to bear the
brunt of the default of delegates in whose
appointment they had no hand. This, however,
is a contingency which, though possible, is hardly
likely to occur.

The sanitary powers which are conferred upon
county councils are twofold. First, they are
intrusted with the power of taking proceedings
to enforce the provisions of the Rivers Pollution
Prevention Act, 1876; and they may not only
take proceedings themselves, but they may con-

tribute towards the cost of proceedings instituted under the Act by any other county council, or by an urban or rural authority. Furthermore, the Local Government Board may by provisional order constitute a joint committee representing all administrative counties through which any river may pass, and that committee may form an independent body of itself to protect a river in question against pollution. The provisions of the Rivers Pollution Prevention Act are pretty well known. They are directed to prevent the pollution of streams either by manufacturers, miners, or even by sanitary authorities themselves. It has not always been found that sanitary authorities are above the temptation of turning their sewage into the nearest available river regardless of the pollution which may be caused. Manufacturers are, however, probably the greatest sinners in this respect, and numerous proceedings under the Act have from time to time been taken in respect of discharges of an offensive or noxious kind from various factories. Much is expected from the extension of the powers under this Act to the county councils. The sanitary authorities who have been offenders could not be expected to prosecute themselves, nor have some of the small sanitary authorities been able or willing to take proceedings against some of the larger and more powerful manufacturers in their districts, who have therefore been allowed to pollute the streams to their hearts' content. The county councils will be independent of immediate local interests, and will, it is hoped, exercise a wise and beneficent jurisdiction in this respect. The other sanitary power conferred on the county councils is that of appointing a medical officer of health. As far as the Act of Parliament

can indicate the intention of the Legislature, it
seems to be desired that the medical officer shall
be one who gives his whole time and attention to
the work of the council, for without the written
consent of the council he is not to engage in
private practice. His services may by arrangement with the county councils be made regularly
available for any district council within the
county, and unless he has had experience as a
medical officer or as an inspector of the Local
Government Board he is to possess certain special
diplomas. The most important enactment in
regard to sanitary matters is, however, that which
requires every medical officer of health for a
district in the county to send to the county
council a copy of his periodical reports, and the
county councils are charged with the duty of
examining such reports, and if it should appear
to them that the Public Health Act has not
properly been put in force within the district to
which the report relates, or that any other matter
affecting the public health of the district requires
to be remedied, councils may cause representation to be made to the Local Government Board
upon the matter. In its present form this is a
very mild power, indeed, to confer on the county
councils, but it may be hoped that a future Act
will considerably extend it.

It may be convenient next to pass to the crowd
of minor matters as to which the powers of
justices are transferred to the county councils.
The Contagious Diseases of Animals Act is to be
administered by the county councils. As the local
authority they will often have to consider
whether a market or a fair should be stopped or
restricted. They will have large powers for
inspection and slaughter—subject to compensation—of diseased animals and animals which

have been in contact with disease or are likely to be infected. They will be able to prohibit the removal of animals and compel disinfection, but they will be subject to a general control on the part of the Privy Council. The county councils are also to act as the local authority under the Destructive Insects Act, but that Act, which was passed in anticipation of the Colorado beetle, has never yet been put in force, and if it should become operative all that the county councils will have to do will be to assess the compensation for any crops, which in order to stamp out the insect, they might direct to be destroyed. The county councils will act as the local authority with regard to fish conservancy, and they will be able to appoint in fishery districts which the Secretary of State may form boards of conservators with power to issue licences, make by-laws as to close time, and generally enforce laws for the protection of fish. Under the Wild Birds Acts the only powers which the county councils appear to have is to make an application to the Secretary of State that the close time for any particular bird may be extended. With regard to weights and measures, the county councils will have to provide legal standards of measure and weight and means for verifying weights and measures by comparison with such standards. They will have to appoint inspectors of weights and measures and allot them districts and make by-laws for regulating their duties and fixing the fees which are to be taken. A set of standard weights and measures costs somewhere about £100, but as every Court of Quarter Sessions possesses a set of standards, and as they will pass to the county councils with the other property transferred by the Act, no fresh expense will be incurred in this respect.

The county councils will also have to protect the public in the use of gas meters. They will take over from the Courts of Quarter Sessions copies of the models of gas meters and will have to appoint inspectors to examine and stamp meters in their respective districts.

Inspectors have to attend in towns where gas is consumed if so required, and are to examine and test and if found correct stamp meters. The Act contemplates that a meter may register more than 2 per cent. in favour of the seller or 3 per cent. in favour of the consumer, but beyond those limits a meter is not to be considered correct. The inspectors have general powers of entering houses and examining meters, and penalties are provided to be enforced where certain standards of correctness are not observed. The county council will have the appointment of an analyst under the Sale of Food and Drugs Acts, and they will be able to prescribe his duty as to obtaining samples from time to time for the purpose of analysis, and the analyst is to make a quarterly report showing the number of articles analyzed by him, the result of each analysis, and the sum paid in respect thereof. Samples may be submitted by the analyst, by any medical officer, inspector of nuisances, inspector of weights and measures, inspector of markets, or police constable. If on the analyst's report it appears that an offence has been committed in respect of any article so submitted the officer submitting it may take proceedings for the recovery of the penalties provided by the Act. As to explosives the county councils will become the local authority. It will be for them to grant licences for premises used for the manufacture and storage of explosives, and to appoint inspectors to keep a careful eye upon those premises. In smaller towns the approach of November 5 is a signal for the increased activity of the explosives inspector, but in the larger towns and in the country districts explosives of more importance than squibs and crackers will engage the attention of the inspectors and of the county councils. The Home Office inspectors of explosives keep a most vigilant watch upon all the local authorities, and are in the habit of paying " surprise " visits to districts. They look up the local inspector, ask him to make a round of inspection in their company and in that way from time to time test the efficiency of the officers appointed by the local authorities. The larger explosive factories have to be licensed directly by the Home Secretary, and the local authorities are free from any responsibility and from inspection or supervision. That the bridges and the roads repairable as bridges should in future be looked after by the county councils instead of the county justices goes almost without saying. That the main roads should be repairable by the county councils is quite a new departure. Hitherto the county authority, while it has had power of supervision and inspection and has had to contribute half the cost of the maintenance of main roads, it has not generally had any duty in regard to their repairs. There are upwards of 17,000 miles of main roads in England, and their repairs come to more than £600,000 in the year. In future those repairs are to be done, and. therefore, that money will have to be spent by the county councils, subject, however, to the provision that an urban authority may, if it please, apply to the county council to be allowed to repair its own main road and it will then devolve upon the urban authority to maintain it, but they will then be able to get from the county council an annual sum towards the expense in which it will be involved. The council will have various highway powers of more or less importance. The authority, however, which now has power or duty to light a road will have the same power or duty in future, and the county councils will not be under any responsibility in connexion therewith. A small duty is placed upon county councils in connexion with the registration of the rules of certain societies. They will have to register the rules of scientific societies and of loan societies, but, as they have no discretionary powers as to the contents of the rules, or, in fact, as to the registration, it is hardly worth while to trouble the county councillor with many remarks on the subject. The councils will have to keep a record of all certified places of worship and also a record of charitable gifts, but these are matters which will be well cared for by the clerks of the peace.

The financial powers of county councils have been dealt with in a general way. It probably only remains to add that, for the purpose of emigration, the county councils may make advances so long as they have a guarantee for the repayment of such advances from any local authority in a county or from the Government of any colony. The debts and liabilities of the quarter sessions or justices or officers incurred for county purposes will pass to the county councils, and, subject to providing accomodation for quarter sessions, they may alter and, with the consent of the Local Government Board, sell any land or buildings that they may so acquire. They have, indeed, with regard to all the county property, almost absolute powers of ownership, subject to providing for the administration of justice and the discharge of county business, and

subject also, in specified cases, to the sanction of
the Local Government Board. Then, to relieve
the county councillors from the personal discharge of more work than they can manage,
limited powers of delegation are given to them,
but they may not delegate the power to raise
money on loan. Powers to make by-laws for the
good rule and government of the county and for
the suppression of certain nuisances are also
vested in the county councils. Similar powers
have for many years been intrusted to town
councils under the Municipal Corporations Act.
There must be at least two-thirds of the whole
number of the council present when the by-laws
are made, and they may not come in force until
40 days after a copy of them has been fixed on the
town-hall in a borough or at " some conspicuous
place " in the county. Formalities are provided
with regard to the allowance or confirmation of
the by-laws, but, unfortunately, every offender
against a by-law is at liberty to contend
that it is unreasonable. The fact that the
by-law has been allowed or confirmed by the
prescribed authority is not even *primâ facie* evidence that is reasonable. Recent instances in
which by-laws have been set at nought and
upset by the Courts have been those aimed at
preventing the processions of the Salvation Army ;
while the latest case reported of a by-law, duly
allowed by the Home Secretary, having been
upset by the Court was one made by the Corpo-
ration of Newcastle-upon-Tyne. The town
council made a by-law prohibiting children
under eight selling articles in the streets at any
time, and prohibiting children under 12 selling
in the streets between 10 o'clock in the evening
and 5 o'clock in the morning. There was no
doubt that the motives of the council were very

laudable, and one of the judges went as far as to say that if the by-laws had gone on to make the offence conditional on the obstruction to traffic being caused he would have been inclined to hold that the by-law was good ; but it was knocked on the head, and is an instance of the anomaly which the Legislature permits and now perpetuates in allowing a council to frame by-laws which,having passed the ordeal of the Home Office, can be upset by the Court.

The coroner for the county will in future be appointed by the county council and not by the freeholders. All the machinery necessary for enabling the district of a coroner to extend into a county borough or beyond the district of the county council is provided, and some of the existing coroners whose duties are adjusted and whose districts are diminished will be entitled to certain compensation.

The powers of the local authority under the Local Stamp Act are transferred to county councils, but this Act is not largely adapted and merely enables certain local fees to be taken by means of stamps instead of money.

The *quasi*-judicial duties which would have dovolved upon the county councils if their powers of licensing for the sale of intoxicating liquors had remained would have been very considerable. As the Act stands, the duties of this class are not of serious importance. Where, hitherto, music and dancing licences have been granted (under any general Act, by quarter sessions those licences will in future be granted by county councils. Hence-forward it will be the county council of London that will decide whether the Westminster Aquarium and places of that class are to have their licences renewed or refused. The Act

under which the London places of amusement
are licensed extends only to 20 miles from the
boundaries of the metropolis. There are, however, local Acts conferring a similar power in
existence in some places, but probably they
would not be considered " General Acts," and
so possibly the transfer by the Local Government
Act of music and dancing licensing to county
councils will extend only to the metropolis and
20 miles round it. The county council are also
to have the powers of the justices to grant
licences for stage plays. As the licences for
theatres in London and places where the
Sovereign occasionally resides are granted by the
Lord Chamberlain and not by justices, the
county councils of London, Windsor, Brighton,
and one or two other places will have nothing to
do with licensing theatres within their districts. Elsewhere the theatrical licences will
in future be granted in the discretion of
the county councils, who can make rules
for insuring order and good behaviour in the
buildings. Further power as to licensing is conferred upon the county councils under the Race
Course Licensing Act, 1879. That Act, however, only applies to such race-courses as are
within 10 miles of Charing-cross, and so will only
affect London and one or two other councils. The
only other duty that can be called *quasi*-judicial
is that which will arise under the Riot (Damages)
Act, 1886. Under that Act compensation for
injury, stealing, or destruction of property caused
by riotous and tumultuous assemblies will be
fixed by the county councils (beyond the Metropolitan Police District) and paid out of the
police rate. In awarding compensation the
council have several matters to take into their
consideration, and particularly as to how far the

claimant actively or passively contributed to his property being damaged.

Besides these various matters other powers will bo exercised by the county councils. They will bo ablo to mako provisional orders for tho compulsory acquirement of land for the purposo of allotments. These powers, however, they aro not likely to bo called upon to exercise, for if tho real valuo of tho land is such as to justify a local authority in buying it thero will generally bo no difficulty in getting tho vendor to sell ; while if tho real value bo such that allotment rents will not rccoup tho expenditure tho local authority will not want to buy, compulsorily or otherwiso. They will also havo power to divido tho county into polling districts for tho purposo of Parliamentary elections, and they will havo a varicty of minor powers and duties which aro all in their turn of moro or less importance, but which need not seriously exerciso tho minds of county councillors.

The brief sketch that has thus been given as to the nomination and candidaturo and election of county councils, and as to somo of their powers and duties, has not been intended to supersedo tho advice which tho county councils will from timo to timo receivo from tho clerks of the peaco or from their other professional advisers. Nor has tho qualification of tho county elector been dealt with. Tho list of electors and of persons qualified to be elected to tho councils had been published when the first paper of this series appeared and tho timo had clapsed for making claims. Theso lists havo now for tho mos part been revised and completed, and they contain tho names of many mcn who livo not for themselves alono. Theso papers may enablo such men to decido whether or not they will join tho ranks of tho county councillors, and if they should become candidates to warn them of some of the dangers which may beset their path in the course of candidature. Considering the enormous number of amendments that were introduced, almost at the last moment, into the Bill as it passed through Parliament, the Local Government Act is even now a model of scientific drafting. It is probable, however, that so complex a piece of legislation will be open to numerous attempts to construe it in a variety of ways, and it is not likely that many months may elapse before the Courts of Law are called upon to interpret several of its provisions.

LEADING ARTICLE, OCTOBER 23.

We print to-day the sixth and concluding article of a series in which an endeavour has been made to explain clearly, succinctly, and compendiously the leading provisions of the Local Government Act as regards both the mode of electing the new County Councillors and the duties which the County Councils will have to undertake as soon as they are fully constituted. A " Vade Mecum "for County Councillors " of this kind, if we may so term it, is all the more necessary and useful because, although the Act is, as our Correspondent says, a model of scientific drafting, it is, for that very reason, perhaps, not drafted in such a form as to be readily understanded of the people. The main principle of the Act is to extend to the counties, and to the boroughs, cities, and municipalities regarded as counties for the purposes of the Act, the system of local organization and government already established in municipal boroughs. This principle has been incorporated in the very structure of the Act, and the practice, so dear to the scientific draftsman, of constructing a new statute by reference to the provisions of an old one has been carried to such an extent that the County Councillor can only attain to a clear conspectus of his functions

and duties by reading the Local Government Act
to which he owes his existence together with the
Municipal Corporations Act, and especially the
second schedule of the latter. For legal and
judicial purposes, and for certain Parliamentary
purposes, this practice is, no doubt, very convenient. Lawyers and Courts of Law always
have copies of the statutes at hand, and
it makes very little difference to them whether
the law is to be found in one volume or a dozen.
For the County Councillor, on the other hand, it
is a little perplexing to find that when he has
mastered the Local Government Act he is only
at the beginning of the studies necessary to
fit him for the discharge of his new duties.
We trust that the exposition of the Act
which we have printed will remove many
of his difficulties. We have already told a
prospective candidate what to do and how to do
it, and also what he must not do, if he wishes to
become a County Councillor ; and in the sixth
article, which we print to-day, and its immediate
predecessor we have explained what he will have
to do when he has attained the object of his
ambition. The only thing now remaining to be
done is for candidates to present themselves.
The lists of electors and of persons qualified to
be elected have now been compiled and
published, but the districts into which counties
are to be divided for the purposes of election
have still in many cases to be defined. That
task, which is intrusted to the Quarter Sessions,

will bo completed early next month, and then
candidates will bo able to declare themselves.
Wo repeat what wo havo already said more than
once, that a great deal will depend on tho class
of men who como forward, and wo earnestly
trust that tho electors will bestir themselves in
all parts of tho country to securo men as their
candidates who will givo to tho County Councils such a character for energy, capacity, and
public spirit as will go far to determino tho
wholo futuro of Local Government in this
country.

A great many preliminary and provisional questions will havo to bo settled when tho County
Councils first meet. Tho Councils themselves
will not bo formally constituted until tho County
Aldermen havo been selected by tho elected
Councillors meeting provisionally for tho purpose;
and as tho selection of tho Aldermen will probably cause somo vacancies among tho elected
Councillors somo further delay will probably
occur in practico, though tho Act does not appear
to require that tho provisional meetings should bo
suspended until tho vacancies havo been filled
up. Wo shall watch with somo interest and
anxiety tho working of tho provisions for tho
election of Aldermen. An Alderman need not bo
selected from among tho elected Councillors, but
ho must possess tho qualifications of an elected
Councillor. Thero is thus a choice between three
classes—namely, elected Councillors, men who have
been unsuccessful at tho poll, and men who,
although qualified, havo not offered themselves as

candidates for popular election. We trust that the
Councillors in choosing Aldermen will endeavour to select men who will add strength,
authority, and even dignity to the Council, rather
than men who, possessing precisely the same
qualifications as themselves, will only add
strength to a party majority on one side or the
other. When the Council is fully constituted, it
will elect its Chairman for the year, and may
determine whether he is to receive remuneration or
not, and will fix the number of its own
meetings. These must be at least four in the
year, of which one is to be held on the 7th of
November, and may be as many as the business
to be transacted requires. The Council will then
nominate its Committees and adjust its relations
with the Court of Quarter Sessions. A joint Committee of the Council and Quarter Sessions is to
have charge of the police and other important
matters ; this Committee will appoint its own
Chairman, who will have a casting vote in all
cases of equality ; and if the votes for two candidates for the office of Chairman are equal, one of
them is to be chosen by lot. It is thus one of
the anomalies of the Act that the decision of
important questions by the joint Committee may
rest upon the casting vote of a Chairman chosen
by lot. Such is the law, and perhaps in practice
it will seldom work amiss ; but the anomaly
is a curious product of the joint wisdom of
Parliament and the Local Government Board
devoted to the creation of a representative

system of Local Government. The next important business of the Councils will be to consider and adjust their financial position and
responsibilities. They will begin life with a
tolerably full exchequer—that is, there is a sum
of over £2,500,000 now received as Grants in Aid
of Local Taxation to be discontinued and a sum
of nearly £5,500,000 derived from licence duties
and other Imperial revenue to be divided among
the County Councils. Against this, on the other
hand, there are the outstanding liabilities of
county finance to be taken over, including a sum
of £2,800,000 for lunatic asylums and of nearly
half a million for police stations and gaols, and
there are besides a variety of liabilities and assets
to be adjusted between the counties and the
boroughs. There is thus plenty of room and need
for financial ability and skill in the County
Councils. It is, perhaps, to be feared that these
qualities may be checked in their development by
the very tight leading-strings imposed by the Act
on the new county finance. No sum exceeding
£50 can be ordered to be spent at any meeting of
the Council unless the notice summoning the
meeting has stated the amount and the purpose
for which the money is required ; and not even £5
can be borrowed without the sanction of the Local
Government Board. The restriction on the
borrowing powers is salutary, at least at the
outset, though it hardly fulfils the promise
of decentralization which was supposed to
be one of the chief recommendations of

the Act. Financial control is the key of the whole situation, and so long as it is retained in the hands of the Local Government Board it is that office of the State, and not the County Councils, that will really be responsible for Local Government. The £50 limit will not be found very inconvenient where the business of the County Council is so considerable as to require frequent meetings, but in the smaller Councils, whose meetings will not perhaps largely exceed the statutory number of four, it may prove a troublesome restriction not altogether conducive to economy. Committees will be apt to fall into the extravagant habit of asking for a larger sum than they immediately need in order to save themselves the trouble and inconvenience of summoning a special meeting to vote money as it is actually required.

The executive duties of the County Councils will be of the highest importance to the community, and they will demand no little public spirit for their punctual and faithful discharge. They are enumerated in the article which we print elsewhere to-day. The Council will take charge of pauper lunatic asylums, of reformatory and industrial schools ; it will be associated with the magistrates in the management of the county police ; it will administer the Rivers Pollutions Act, and will be empowered to appoint a medical officer of health, who may be required to abstain from private practice and to devote his whole time to the duties assigned to him by the Council ;

it will repair county bridges and main roads ; and will exercise a large variety of minor powers which need not here be specified. Before we see the County Councils actually at work it is difficult to anticipate with any approach to accuracy the direction in which the transfer of power from the hands of the magistracy to that of a representative body will first manifest itself in any decided change of policy or result. There is, undoubtedly, room for improvement in the management of pauper lunatic asylums, and the County Councils will certainly be expected to ascertain for themselves whether the ribs and breastbones of lunatics—especially pauper lunatics—are quite so brittle as they are sometimes represented to be, and why it is that lunatics—especially pauper lunatics—are so very apt to tumble into over-heated baths. In the administration and enforcement of the Rivers Pollution Acts, again, the County Councils are likely to prove stronger and more exacting than local sanitary authorities have been, though here it must be recollected that manufacturers who find it convenient to pour their refuse into the nearest rivers will be very apt to seek a place on the County Councils and to endeavour to persuade their colleagues that their particular refuse is the most harmless substance in the world. In sanitary matters it is to be expected that the County Councils will be neither much more nor much less enlightened than the constituencies to which they will owe their existence. Probably more attention is now paid to sanitary science in England than in any other country in the world, but there is still plenty of room for improvement even in England; and we suspect that, if the whole truth were known, there is quite as much room for improvement in rural England as there is in urban England. In towns self-interest almost compels us to be sanitary, the penalty for indulgence in insanitary conditions is so heavy and so certain to be exacted sooner or later. In rural districts, on the other hand, the mischief is more insidious and less palpable, though not less destructive in proportion to the sparser population. There is plenty of room, therefore, for the energies of a County Council in the development of rural sanitation. On the whole, the duties of a County Councillor, though not exciting in themselves, and not attractive to every one, should be of sufficient importance to induce good men and good citizens to undertake their discharge. If the Local Government Act failed to quicken the civic life of our rural districts and to raise it to higher levels of virtue, capacity, integrity, and intelligence, then, indeed, we should have to admit that representative institutions themselves are on their trial.

PRINTED AND PUBLISHED BY GEORGE EDWARD WRIGHT,
AT THE TIMES OFFICE, PRINTING-HOUSE SQUARE,
LONDON.

www.ingramcontent.com/pod-product-compliance
Lightning Source LLC
Chambersburg PA
CBHW031441270326
41930CB00007B/823